# Breaking into Advertising

## how to market yourself like a professional

**Jeanette Smith**

Peterson's
Princeton, New Jersey

Visit Peterson's Education Center on the Internet (World Wide Web) at www.petersons.com

Copyright © 1998 by Peterson's

**Library of Congress Cataloging-in-Publication Data**
Smith, Jeannette (Jeannette H.)
    Breaking into advertising : how to market yourself like a professional / Jeannette Smith.
        p.    cm.
    Includes index.
    ISBN 0-7689-0122-7
    1. Advertising—Vocational guidance.   2. Job hunting.   I. Title.
HF5828.4.S57   1998
659.1'023'73—dc21                                                      98-30192
                                                                            CIP

Printed in the United States of America
10 9 8 7 6 5 4 3 2 1

# contents

# section

## The Ad Business and the Roads to Get There

Right here, right now, you have a choice to make: Which chapters of this book will you use, and which will you skip?

*First Choice.* If you're a newcomer to advertising, with little or no groundwork in the subject, be sure to read Chapters 1 through 4. They will give you the basics about advertising you need if you're to have any hope of breaking into the business . . . whether it's merely to find a job or to begin a career.

*Second Choice.* If you are reasonably knowledgeable about the industry, or if you have an advertising or marketing degree, you can skip Section I and go directly to Section II.

*Third Choice.* If you're already a member of this relatively small "fraternity," if you've already broken into the field, looked around, and now believe it's the place you want to be and it's the right time to move up the ladder—or if you'd like to take a shot at moving into another area of advertising—go directly to Section III. After you've read Chapters 13 and 14, however, go back through Section II to get the help necessary to accomplish your new goal.

# chapter 1

## The Ad Business

*Advertising!* We're so used to seeing it just about everywhere, we rarely stop to think about its influence, its power, or its force in shaping our values and desires and altering the way we view what is going on in the world. "It's come to the point where people look to advertising to see how they feel about themselves," says psychologist Carol Moog.

Although recognition of this power is relatively new, it is strong enough that most in the business have jumped on the bandwagon to join in playing the influence tune. "Taking a cue from real life, Madison Avenue is carefully crafting images that shape our attitudes about ourselves, our relationships and our material needs," reports *Advertising Age*. "You might say advertising holds a mirror up to society," says Michael Marsden, professor of pop culture at Bowling Green State University. "It defines, distills, shapes, and focuses our basic values in a very powerful way," he says.

Of course, the ongoing basic challenge that is at the heart of all advertising is to solve a problem. This could be a marketing problem, a sales problem, or an image problem.

## HOW DO YOU DEFINE ADVERTISING?

Have you ever asked someone for a definition of the Internet? Or just a simple, understandable explanation of what it is and how it works? If you thought that was difficult, try getting definitions of marketing and advertising. And an explanation of what they are, what they do, and how—or whether—they're related.

Odds are you'll hear that advertising is the same as marketing. Even among the pros, marketing and advertising have pretty much become synonymous. Long-established, well-known advertising agencies now are calling themselves marketing agencies. Although most dictionaries don't quite agree either on exactly what advertising and marketing are, and what each does, The American Marketing Association, at least, has a formal definition of marketing:

> Marketing is the process of planning and executing the conception, pricing, promotion, and distribution of ideas, goods, and services to create exchanges that will satisfy individual and organizational objectives.

Mark N. Clemente, in his book *The Marketing Glossary* (AMACOM Books, 1992), recognizes that marketing is a "complex, interrelated series of activities." He explains these activities with a list of four distinct processes: (1) developing the product or service, (2) establishing a price for it, (3) communicating information about it through various direct and indirect communications channels, and (4) coordinating its distribution to ensure product accessibility by target buyers.

Clemente's four-part definition clearly shows that marketing comprises totally different processes and that advertising is only one part of marketing—the number three process that communicates information through various direct and indirect communications channels. When Clemente turns his discussion toward a definition of advertising, he points out that it "involves using *paid* media to communicate persuasive information about a product, service, organization, or idea." That distinction separates advertising from publicity, a service that, along with public relations, has also become a division of advertising agencies.

So let's get this point straight right from the beginning: Advertising is *not* marketing. There are more than a hundred slices of the marketing pie, which can include a logo and slogan for the business, business cards and letterhead, packaging for the product, a sign for the delivery truck, brochures, promotions, annual reports, and so on. It is true that advertising is an *integral part* of marketing—the most visible and most recognized part—but advertising is a strong enough subject to stand on its own.

Does that get us off on the right foot? We don't want to invite problems of misunderstandings or cause confusion by using the two words interchangeably as you go about breaking into this exciting, challenging, fulfilling business of *advertising*.

## THE POWER OF ADVERTISING

"Advertising is the most efficient known way of moving goods in practically every product class," advertising icon Leo Burnett told those attending the fiftieth anniversary celebration of the American Association of Advertising Agencies (AAAA). He also reminded them that advertising makes possible our unparalleled variety of magazines, newspapers, business publications, and radio and television stations. "Without advertising we would have a far different nation, and one that would be much poorer—not merely in material commodities, but in the life of the spirit," he told the AAAA gathering.

Advertising has unique strengths, and one of its greatest is that it builds strength. It helps solve the problems that challenge business and governments. Even in the worst of times there has been a need to sell products and build brand names. Advertising has had a strong part in rebuilding the U.S. economy when it has slumped or crashed. The United States leads the world in the skill and mastery of advertising techniques that accelerate economic growth and continue to raise living standards.

If you want to measure the importance of advertising, *Advertising Age* suggests you look around your home at the products you use every day. "Think about the advertising that goes into building those brands—and what those brands have done for their companies, their workers, shareholders, and factory towns, not to mention your media and your lifestyle." It suggests you "focus on one product. Understand, say, how Crest fluoride toothpaste affected the dentifrice market, the dental profession, our lives, and the lives of our children. And then try to square it with the notion that advertising is a drain on the economy."

## ADVERTISING'S ECONOMIC INFLUENCE

One more thing you may not have paid much attention to is advertising's *economic* influence. This influence is ignored mainly because it is almost impossible to measure accurately.

Advertising notable and author S. William Pattis points out in his book *Careers In Advertising* (VGM Career Horizons, 1996) that advertising plays an important part in the distribution of goods and services. "The demand created by advertising helps the economy grow by stimulating demands for products. Of course, the cost of advertising is reflected in the cost of the product, but advertisers believe that advertising creates extra sales, and product pricing can be reduced as a result of increased production."

## AN INVESTMENT OR AN EXPENSE?

The issue of whether to consider advertising an investment or an expense is where our discussion gets a little sticky, because the answer depends on who you're talking to. Advertising and marketing people typically view advertising as an investment, although they acknowledge that the money spent may not show a direct or exact dollar return amount. They claim that when advertising builds a firm base for a product or service over time, nonbuyers may feel goodwill toward both the product or service and the company that sells it. That's an asset, advertisers maintain, that turns a profit even when it can't be calculated in a dollar amount. Accountants and finance persons, on the other hand, claim that advertising is a direct expense that should be charged against the operation of a company and the manufacture and sale of its product.

Northwestern University professor Don E. Schultz wrote in his book *Strategic Advertising Campaigns* (National Textbook Company, 1990) that "Presently, federal and state governments regard advertising as an expense item. That is, the money invested in advertising is taken as an expense deduction in the period in which it was used, and, for accounting purposes, is considered a cost of doing business."

## THE STORY OF ADVERTISING

Many people think of advertising, along with marketing, as something that has been developed in recent years. Instead, it goes back to at least 3000 B.C. Babylon, where signs were used by vendors to show shoppers pictures of the product or service offered. Town criers announced the arrival of ships and what was available in their cargoes. Later, one man changed life for all time: Johannes Gutenberg, inventor of the first movable type printing press, was the real facilitator of advertising. Almost immediately after his invention newspapers and magazines began printing, and profiting from, advertising. That was early in the fifteenth century. In the United States, advertising found its place during the American Revolution (1775–1783) and hasn't slowed since. At that time, merchants wrote and placed their own advertising in local publications. About the middle of the nineteenth century newspaper and magazine publishers woke up to the fact this could be a major source of revenue and commissioned agents to sell advertising to manufacturers and retailers.

## THE BIRTH OF ADVERTISING AGENTS

Unfortunately, the first agents weren't always the most reputable people around. They were hired and paid by publishers rather than advertisers and so handled the ads to benefit publishers rather than advertisers—or product consumers. They thereby earned themselves somewhat unsavory reputations.

It wasn't until the late 1860s that someone showed up on the scene to ultimately change the entire advertising system. His name was N. W. Ayer, and it was his belief that he should represent the interests of advertisers. He put together a crew of creative people including artists and writers and proceeded to convince advertisers that he would work for *their* best interests. Thus was born the first model of a contemporary advertising agency. Today, advertising agencies represent only their clients and do not work for media.

Following that major change came another development where advertisers set up their own in-house "agencies." They, too, exist in full bloom today, some with complete staffs to handle the entire process, others tapping into resource groups for many of the services they require, such as writing and production. Still others continue to hire agencies to do all or part of the process. Large corporations usually use a combination of methods. They may be represented by one or more agencies but have an in-house advertising department to serve as the conduit between management and each agency and to work closely with the agency. Some advertising departments also perform part of the process themselves.

## THE INFO-DRIVEN MARKETING FUTURE

"Marketing is being revolutionized by the onrush of new and more sophisticated information-technology tools," shouts *Advertising Age* in a four-part series. Smart advertising agents are using these tools to gain competitive advantage "via the savvy use of information-powered marketplace strategies and tactics. We can do things with computers that made no economic sense five years ago, and we will be doing things with them in five years that make no sense today," says Stephan H. Haecket, director of strategic studies at IBM, in the *Advertising Age* series.

The results of computer technology are evident in the ability to identify customers "who have the highest profit-improvement potential and to use databases to understand the specific needs of those subsegments," says Alan W. H. Grant, founder of the Boston-based consultants Exchange Partners in *Advertising Age*. Grant adds, "Essentially the only data available in the past to a supermarket chain consisted of aggregated sales figures for the various items it carried. Today, however, careful analysis of the detailed data gathered via supermarket frequent-shopper programs can provide valuable information not only about customer segments and specific purchase behaviors. It also can be cross-correlated to the bottom-line impact of those shopping activities."

These findings can help retailers create special advertising programs that precisely target a specific purchase behavior and a narrowly defined customer segment. Not only new technology is pounding on the doors of advertisers and their agents, but it's arguably the most important development in the advertising world.

So, why is this important to *you?* The answer is simple: If you don't board the new-tech train you'll be left at the depot.

## NEW ON MADISON AVENUE

Maybe the new technology of satellites and computers has opened minds and made ad agencies more adventuresome. The greatest in the business are the ones able and willing to hold up a new-tech mirror to society to give their public exactly what they want instead of just laying out a product for the masses. These segmented publics reward the advertiser by buying the product.

One new concept on Madison Avenue—which has become synonymous with advertising's cream of the crop—is "reality" ads, both in print and on TV. In reality ads, advertisers acknowledge consumers' attitudes and values by presenting images by which consumers can measure themselves. Psychologists explain the concept as people's need to look to advertising to see how they match up, which, in turn, affects how they feel about themselves. Those who are successful in advertising today are those able to perceive what people believe. They become increasingly successful because they stay aware of what people want and then give it to them.

## WHAT'S AHEAD FOR ADVERTISING AND BUSINESS?

You'd think that the surge in high-tech development calls for many changes in advertising, perhaps even the elimination of advertising as we know it today. Not so, say those who spend their lives analyzing developments.

Marketers agree that "technology, both in products and in communication delivery systems, is going to play a greater role in the future," reports *Advertising Age*. But advertising is going to play an important role in the twenty-first century. And its content and delivery will change only with the changing marketplace.

Media is becoming more fragmented; the era of network TV dominance appears to be almost over. Ordering goods via home computer certainly will play a greater role in the twenty-first century. However, many executives agree that consumers' needs in the next century are not going to differ tremendously from those of today.

Here's a tip about one area of the advertising business you may want to break into. An *Advertising Age* report states, "Many of us have been dealing in categories and businesses [in which] there hasn't been much going on in terms of real product differentiation. But that's going to have to change. We're going to have to spend a lot more money on *research and development* to make breakthrough products [and to get those products to the right buyers' groups]." Emphasis will increase on the research behind identifying who the customers are and what their buying habits are in order to make the personal one-to-one contact that new tech has made so easy. If you love research, that's a division within the field that will stay very active as long as advertising is around.

## ADVERTISING IS EVERYWHERE!

As reported earlier, experts agree that advertising is going to play an important role in the twenty-first century. They neglect to mention, however, that its role has already increased in terms of the numbers and kinds of places where advertising now appears.

Here's a challenge. Try to come up with a type of space that doesn't offer ad space. Advertising is everywhere—even in the craziest places! "There no longer are any ad-free zones," reported the *Dallas Morning News* in it's 1998 first-of-the-year report. "The rush is on to follow people everywhere and nail them when they least expect it." For example, there's a company in Richardson, Texas, that offers "personalized seating products"—ads placed in the space atop chairs and leather bar stools. And they boast some impressive clients—Pepsi, Amoco, GM Goodwrench, Ford, Honda, Pennzoil, and Motorola, to name just a few.

There are screens and speakers on convenience store gas pumps. Ads on rooftop watertanks, on cabs, buses and bus shelters, trash baskets, parking meters, and on the shopping bags full of purchases you made at the mall. Ads in movie theaters are old hat but relatively new on school buses and in locker rooms. Schools in Grapevine, Texas, receive $3 million for ads placed on school building roofs, apparently so airplanes overhead get a message!

There is little doubt that ads are coming soon to your ATM machine, if they are not there already. "While the machines are scratching their heads or whatever it is they do for a while before giving you your money," reports *U.S. News & World Report* writer John Leo, "a TV-type ad comes on and pushes some merchandise." Initially there was a problem when customers rebelled because the ad played for 30 seconds. That's been worked out; now they play for only 15 seconds. Talk about captive audiences! Electronic Data Systems, which introduced the technology, gets right to the point: "You have a very captive consumer; they're just staring at the screen."

Perhaps the most eye-popping in this POP (point of purchase) world is the newest place for advertising—on navigational screens in high-end luxury cars. *Advertising Age*'s editor-in-chief Rance Crain predicts, "The navigation systems are destined to become a key reason to buy a particular auto make, and car marketers will vie with one another to provide enhanced 'concierge' services as part of the navigation setup." The advertising possibilities for these in-car navigation systems are endless. Crain gives some examples: "McDonald's Corp. could send out CDs to car owners with the locations of its outlets programmed into the route structure. Movie theaters will also want to show their locations. Press the theater icon and you'll get what movies are showing and when they start." As he says, the possibilities are endless.

## ADVERTISING'S INTEGRITY

Back in the early days of advertising, the "pitchmen" weren't repressed by regulations or ordinances. Ultimately they gave the business a bad reputation that still lingers to some degree to this day. Extravagant promises still make it into print and broadcast ads. But the public is hugely wary, and, with one-to-one computer shopping, the public now is able to demand honesty and reliability in online advertising.

Also, there is Federal Trade Commission (FTC) regulation and monitoring to determine whether an ad is false or misleading. If proof of questionable claims cannot be produced, the FTC can order the removal of advertising. Within the industry are associations that discourage and penalize improper or unethical advertising. Some, such as the AAAA, have created codes. Everyone who works in the field should be totally aware of advertising's ethics, responsibilities, and restrictions.

## ADVERTISING'S DIM BULBS OUTSHONE BRIGHT LIGHTS

On the next-to-last day of 1997 the *New York Times* did a roundup of good and bad ads. The headline stated that it had been "A Year of Risks As Turbulence Stirs Creativity" and went on to say that some agencies' disregard for rules yielded "some noble failures" but that lots of ads hit pay dirt. Stuart Elliott, the *Times*'s highly respected advertising analyst, said that the turmoil in advertising ("abrupt account changes, surprising personnel shifts, disruptive deals and consolidations") indicated that advertising was taking more risks, breaking more rules, and showing more spunk. "Now and then you have to go way out on a limb to pick the sweetest fruit," was the way Elliott explained it. If Elliott is right about the causes, then there's no let up in sight into the new millennium.

The point of the article was to name the best and the worst ads, and the reason for including examples is for the lessons they offer. However, Elliott said, "the failures were so egregious that for this year's list, the pans precede the praise." One of the "dim bulbs" listed was a commercial for the sporty Cadillac Catera. It offended the very people it was meant to charm, says Elliott. It was intended to be a humorous sendup of fairy tales, but few, if any, viewers got the joke, "distracted as they were by the supermodel Cindy Crawford in an outré leather outfit that screamed Sexism!' "

A Holiday Inn commercial was another example of a missed opportunity, according to Stuart Elliott. The most alluring woman at a 1975 class reunion turns out to have once been named Bob; the makeover is likened to an overhaul of the Holiday Inn chain. "But the final shot saws off the limb onto which the spot's creators crawled out, as a male classmate reacts to the made-over Bob with disgust." Elliott observes that a far better ending would have been for the classmate to become intrigued enough to rush the former Bob off to the nearest Holiday Inn.

Visa Check Card was given a pat on the back. One of two of their "bright light" commercials offers an intelligent twist to the old joke about someone who is well-known being asked for identification to cash a check. One features Bob Dole and, as Elliott says, "has earned him a second career as a TV pitchman."

The attempt by Mercedes-Benz to radically revamp its image among younger Americans is working because of its unconventional advertising "imbued with humor, music, and emotion," says Elliott.

## THE MAJOR NEWS IS SAVED FOR LAST

You're entitled, having read this far, to the biggest news of the chapter: There's a talent shortage!

No less an authority than the president of AAAA, O. Burtch Drake, said "There's a real talent shortage. Agencies are having a harder and harder time attracting bright talent because of the appeal of higher-paying careers like investment banking and because programs to recruit newcomers to the advertising industry were cut back during the last recession."

If that news doesn't make your day, what will? As a matter of fact, ad agencies are so hard up that job applicants with talent and passion for the business are asking for, and getting, signing bonuses!

So how long will all this last? It's true to some degree that advertising agencies are rooted in the ups and downs of the economy. But the economy doesn't seem to be going anywhere but up. And the advertising business seems to be an economic phenomenon that will continue upward, mainly for two reasons. Because there are more and more new products and services—ranging from unbelievably productive drugs to new-tech inventions—the essential need to get the word out about them, along with the increase in competitiveness in existing products and services, increases ad spending. Add to those reasons one of the great things about this business—in good times, people want to advertise; in bad times, they have to.

An indication of where advertising is going economically came in January 1998. Robert J. Coen, senior vice president and forecasting director at The McCann-Erickson Advertising Agency in New York, estimated that 1998 ad spending would total a record $198.4 billion, up from his estimate for 1997 of $186.8 billion. A report in the December 1997 issue of *Advertising Age* said that agencies are complaining that the brightest entry-level talent is no longer coming their way, "heading instead for Wall Street or taking a run at the interactive media and software businesses." Some believe that ongoing reports of agency downsizing may be a reason there has been such a lack of talent. But a hole is knocked in that excuse, because Wall Street downsized, too.

How long will the splurge in ad spending last? In the business world it's a seller's market during economic good times, but there are hard times when the economy dozes off. In the advertising business, however, whether the economy is up or down, "dedicated, passionate talent" will always be needed.

# chapter 2
## A Review of Advertising 101

It's a whole new world today, where advertising is repeatedly called "marketing" and where new technology is taking over. We all know what advertising is—we think! So why do so many people, even professional advertising people, call it marketing? After all, advertising has been around for centuries, but marketing is a word that, aside from heading to the nearest grocery store with the family's "market list," we've heard used so widely only in recent years.

No one's quite sure who started the confusion and how the two terms became almost interchangeable. We do know that marketing was born when those trying to sell products and services added additional ways to get the products or services recognized, promoted, purchased, sold, and remembered. Or when they set out to develop a new product or service they believed or hoped was wanted or needed.

Advertising is one of the chief elements in marketing. But it is only one part of marketing's complex, interrelated set of functions and activities.

Early in the 1990s, research studies were turning up evidence that a careful blending of media advertising and promotion to support a brand effectively and foster brand loyalty was working. From there, apparently, the blending of all marketing features took off. In 1997, McCann-Erickson Worldwide announced it was changing its name "to reflect the goal of raising other marketing disciplines to the level of traditional advertising." The new name—McCann-Erickson World Group—reflects consolidation of the fourteen companies it has acquired since it began expanding its marketing operations outside of general advertising, each focused on a different channel of marketing. These marketing disciplines include direct marketing, sales promotion, event marketing, brand consultancy, digital media, and public relations.

## THERE ARE ONLY TWO PARTS TO ADVERTISING

As complex as it all seems, advertising has only two parts, media and creative, says Don E. Schultz, adman and professor. Actually, this should be clarified, too. Whereas there are only two parts to *advertising*, there are other segments of *the advertising business*. Therefore, *the business* offers more than just media and creative jobs. We'll get into that later, though.

To return to the idea of advertising as a concept, Schultz points out in his book, *Essentials of Advertising Strategy* (NTC Publishing Group, 1998), that the concept is really quite simple. It's the doing that becomes complex. Further, even though advertising is usually evaluated on the basis of sales, that should not be so, says Schultz, because there are so many factors in the selling process over which advertising has no control. It should be evaluated only on the basis of its communication effects.

## THREE ASSIGNMENTS

The three fundamental assignments for advertising are: to inform consumers about products and their uses, to persuade them to buy the product, and to remind them they need it and the reasons they should continue buying it. This can mean overlaps to some degree of advertising and marketing.

To those outside the business, however, advertising means different things to different people. To a mother getting children ready for a new school year, it may mean a local store ad for pants, tops, and underclothes. To the kids, it may mean finding what movie is playing Saturday at the nearest theater or locating where Nikes, a backpack, or a popular style of bike are on sale. To their father who operates his own business, it may mean getting information about upgrading the company's computer system and finding a store that offers dependable bargain equipment.

## Different Types

Of course, there are many types of advertising: retail, national, trade, industrial, comparison forms, image, and more. Retail advertisers say, "You can buy this product at my store." National advertisers tell you you can buy it anywhere in the country. Trade advertisers say, "Buy this product to sell in your store, and so on."

As one professional tells it, "The different forms of advertising might broadly be characterized by the way in which they seek to encourage the flow of goods."

## Advertising Works for More Than Just Products

Obviously, advertising is used for more than just products. The second major use is by services. Doctors, lawyers, and public service chiefs use it, along with airlines, hotels, insurance, and real estate companies. And of course it's a major tool for politicians. Then there's image advertising, where a product, company, or service tries to build a favorable image, create a new image, or change an outdated or damaged image.

## The Media Mix Is Far-Reaching

When advertising first kicked off in the United States, the only media available were the town crier and a tiny newspaper that was more like a newsletter. Today advertisers have a bewildering number of media choices—newspapers, magazines, outdoor boards, radio, television, cable, direct mail, Yellow Pages, fax, the Internet, and all those weird ad spaces that are coming on the market almost daily—like the tops of bar stools!

New tech has reared its lovely head and made making choices much more complex. But it's also making the end results far more attractive, pleasing, and appealing. For example, newspapers now are digitally enhanced for clearer, cleaner, sharper type and artwork. Ads to be placed in them can be produced and instantly transmitted on the Internet to the designated newspaper. New tech has made two-way, one-to-one advertising not only possible, but popular.

## A Reminder

As you read through the remainder of this chapter, keep in mind that all of this information relates directly to your efforts to break into advertising. The strategies, the steps to accomplishment, and, most important, the tips and techniques for copywriters— particularly if you're seeking work *other* than copywriting—are all useful and applicable to your job search campaign.

## THE IMPORTANCE OF ADVERTISING STRATEGY

Before an advertising campaign can become a campaign, those who develop it must decide what is to be accomplished—what its goals are and what the objectives and strategies are that will accomplish them. (Information about developing goals and objectives is included in Chapter 5.) It is strategies we're concerned with here.

If, say, our intent is to make X percent of our target audience (the potential employers) aware of our product (ourself), and/or if we must establish a purpose or purposes for our product (how we can benefit the employer), and/or if we must create desire or establish need for our product, then we must determine what strategies are required to accomplish these goals. It's far more fun to just start writing an ad or creating the graphics and storylines for a storyboard for a commercial than to sit down and develop the strategies needed to ensure a successful, productive campaign. Strategies require thinking and planning. It's not hard to spot ads and commercials created by people who were not really thinking, apparently for fear they might wear out their brains or use up their creative abilities!

Schultz gives us a basic definition of an advertising strategy: "The formulation of an advertising message that communicates the benefit or problem-solution characteristics of the product or service to the market." He explains that the key words here are "benefit or problem solution characteristics." It's as simple as the fact that if the strategy used doesn't fill a consumer need, solve a consumer problem, or offer a desired consumer benefit, it will fail. Further, all this must be important to the consumer, not to the advertiser.

## Three Steps To Accomplishment

It sounds so simple. "Advertising consists of three steps: (1) getting the right message (2) to the right audience (3) at the right time," says Schultz. And advertising strategy has to do with the first step, developing the "right message."

The basic ingredients for a sound advertising strategy, according to Schultz, are:

1. The strategy must offer a *consumer* benefit or solve a *consumer* problem.
2. The benefit offered or the solution promised must be wanted or desired by the *consumer*.
3. The brand must be tied directly to the benefit or the problem solution offered.
4. The benefit or problem solution must be communicable through media advertising.

There you have the basic basics. (The first three directly relate to your break-in plan. The fourth also relates if you eliminate the last three words, "through media advertising.")

Let's go on and look at how to bring it all about. In insider's jargon, this step is called planning and concepting.

## CONCEPTING COMES FIRST

The basic idea for a campaign, a product, a promotion, or other effort is considered the concept. The research that's required to test reaction to the idea is called *concept testing*. Without the idea there is no campaign. Without concept testing you may waste time, effort, and money on something that won't work. Finding that essential idea almost always comes from brainstorming, either by a group or, if no group is available, by the individual.

As we say in our book *The New Publicity Kit* (John Wiley & Sons, 1995), "Brainstorming is the stretch before a planning exercise." Although brainstorming is often given other names, it is an essential part of establishing goals and of "concepting" for a client. It's a creative process, as is advertising. As a future member of an advertising team, and especially now as an advertising job seeker, it will pay you to learn and use brainstorming.

We've added an easily referenced, easily accessible section in Chapter 8 about the how-tos of brainstorming.

## The Genius of Creativity

This may be a good time to think about creativity and the creative process. Many believe creativity is a talent essential to working in any part of advertising, but this is not so if the work is in the areas of office management, accounting, media buying, traffic, research, or financial management. Understanding and respecting creativity is essential however—after all, advertising is considered one of the "creative fields."

Janean Chun does a great job of setting our feet on the right path to respecting creativity. In an article in *Entrepreneur* magazine, she says, "We all start at the same spot; a blank space [that is to become an ad]—and with a common goal: to fill that space. But the path we choose from there is completely individual, as individual, in fact, as the mind itself. What occupies that distance between nothing and something is the mysterious science we call creativity."

Ronald Scharbo, an advertising professional who has contributed to *Advertising Career Directory*, separates those who work in the field into two categories: right-brain types or left-brain types. He describes right-brainers as "creative visionaries [who] usually start as copywriters and art directors." Left-brainers, he says, are "the disciplined, logical thinkers—the number crunchers. . . . The amazing thing about the agency business is that these two very different types must somehow come together to produce one successful campaign." If there isn't a melding, there's domination by one or the other. The results, Scharbo indicates, are that "left-brain agencies turn out ads that are smart, but dull—strategy statements in print. It's advertising likely to go unnoticed. On the other hand, right-brain agencies turn out ads that are arresting to look at, but don't seem to really say anything."

You've undoubtedly noticed both types of ads—and wondered! Scharbo's observations confirm the need for both types of people in this exciting, stimulating field. And equally important is the undisputed need for both to be able to team up and work together in order to create *effective* advertising—advertising that works.

## NOW FOR THE PLAN

Business people are told, "Don't even *think* about seeking financing without a solid business plan." The same advice with a couple of word changes goes for would-be advertisers: Don't even *think* about advertising without a solid advertising plan. Change a few more words and it's critical advice for you: Don't even *think* about attempting to break into advertising without a solid plan.

That step in the process is covered in Chapter 8. It points out that positioning is the first step in both the advertising planning process as well as in your plan. The entire chapter can be used as a refresher course covering planning as it's done in advertising, but most importantly, it also shows how to develop a creative strategy for your break-in plan.

## THE BASICS OF COPYWRITING

Copywriting is the infrastructure of advertising. Advertising can be successful with words alone. Rarely if ever, however, can an ad accomplish its goal without words.

Probably 80 percent or more of advertising consists of words. These appear in the form of headlines, as the "grabber graf" (catchy paragraph) that kicks off the body copy of an ad to tell the selling features, and in a close that is meant to make the reader take action. Yet this fundamental activity is pretty much ignored in many ad organizations' daily concerns. They may worry about production, design, management, they may worry about everything *but* words.

Sometimes writers overuse words, forgetting that big words can result in less meaning. They forget that simplicity in writing is admired by all, including the most highly educated. They also forget that ambiguous, unfamiliar words may not be understood and possibly may be resented by the very people they are trying to convince. A notice in the window of the Greasy Skillet in one of Jerry Van Amerongen's "Ballard Street" cartoons demonstrates the point. The sign says "Temporarily closed for conceptual enhancement." Without doubt, Greasy Skillet patrons understand the first two words—temporarily closed—but could care less about the reason, even if they comprehend the words.

## Worthy of Your Attention

For all these reasons, copywriting deserves substantial attention, but there's another reason for giving it extra attention here. The basics of copywriting are the basics of good writing, that is, convincing writing. No matter which area of the advertising business you break into—joining either right or left brainers—your *written* words will pave the way to get you the chance to make your pitch, to relate the benefits and advantages you can offer to a particular advertising organization. If you use basics, you will put more energy, vigor, and selling power into the words you use in your letters, your presentation, and all of your "leave-behind" materials—and it will help you better understand the challenges that live with copywriters.

## Writing: Creativity or Craft?

Writing had better be both creativity and craft. For unless you can *think creatively* and sense what needs to be written about and what you want to write about, what you write won't be of much use.

Once you get to the actual writing—that is *craft*. If the topic of how to write could be summed up in two sentences, the formula would be: Get it right. Write it tight.

## At a Loss for Words? Good!

Shorter is better in writing, whether it's an ad, a news story in your favorite newspaper, or a job presentation. But short doesn't necessarily mean good. Paula LaRocque, an assistant managing editor of the *Dallas Morning News* and the newspaper's writing coach, points out in her newspaper column that a writer's work doesn't become better just because it got shorter. "It became *shorter* because it just so happens that the same devices that make writing taut, speedy, and emphatic also shorten it. Compression, not merely cutting, is the real goal." We add that clarity comes through conciseness. Core meaning is achieved by streamlining.

Some of LaRocque's guidelines, though aimed to make newswriting better, are equally applicable to copywriting—and to the preparation of query letters and your presentation package. LaRocque's guidelines are as follows:

- Beginnings: Get right to the point. Avoid beginning with subject-delaying dependent clauses, awkwardly presented anecdotes, and boring scene setters.
- Sentences: Give sentences strong beginnings and endings, and bury weaker material in the sentence's middle. See that every sentence grows out of the sentence preceding it.
- Words: Use small words when you can. Choose the right word, and cut deadwood, redundancies, and vague qualifiers (such as *very, really, truly, quite*).
- Lose prepositions: Use one active verb rather than a group of words that say the same thing. (No—Provide a summary of your proposal; Yes—Summarize your proposal; No—Make an effort; Yes—Try.)
- Phrasing: Avoid saying the obvious. The only thing you can *nod* is your head. The only thing you can *shrug* is your shoulders. The only place *tears* appear is in the eyes.

Now, here's advice from LaRocque to tack up next to your keyboard where you'll see it everytime you draft a piece of writing: "No work is too long that we read happily to its end. And no work is short enough that we read without pleasure."

## Wonder—full!

When it comes to wooing customers, flattery will get you everywhere. Putting a flattering, positive spin on customers' actions usually pays off. (It works with employers, too.) Not the sticky, gooey stuff that sounds artificial but something that will turn indifference or indecision into positives. If what you put in an ad sounds too good to be true, they'll probably rightly believe that it is. But using a headline that plays to the customer's intelligence, perceptiveness, shrewdness, judgment, or prudence can pay off. No one minds these kinds of implications, and the implication can kindle the desire to try whatever is offered.

The state of California tried a different way. They used humor in an effort to break the positive rule. When there was an El Niño–style flood of companies leaving for other states, California decided to initiate an ad campaign aimed at persuading businesses to stay put. The campaign poked fun at Texas, Arizona, and Nevada, states that were luring the businesses away. One ad was headlined "Why Texas Is Telling Tall Tales About California." The focus of the ad was that the states were trying to seduce California businesses with reminders of an "unmerciful mother nature" and economic problems. "What they don't mention is their own subzero weather, alternating with three-shower-a-day humidity along with hurricanes, tornadoes, floods, and mosquitoes that require runways to land," the ad says. The closing graf reads: "You'll need big boots to wade through all the promises that states like Texas are making to Californians. What they still haven't promised, though, is a surefire way to fit a gun rack on a convertible."

Even with the humorous approach, officials were annoyed. The campaign apparently initiated a flood of calls from out-of-state people who were thinking about moving to Texas. Not exactly the result California was hoping for!

## Stretch the Truth a Little!

No big deal, right? Wrong! True, stretching is a part of exercising. But not *this* exercise. Perhaps you've noticed a growing inclination toward seemingly unbelievable capabilities of a product, especially in TV commercials. (Incidentally, it's easier to achieve truth-stretching on radio or TV because consumers have no hard-copy words to check when incredulity strikes.) The headline for a cable advertising conference ad strips away any doubt about its message:

> To Cut It in This Business, You Need a
> REALITY CHECK.

The copy offers truths and benefits, without exaggeration.

> You've got to reexamine your perceptions in this new media landscape, because things are no longer what they once appeared to be.

Then it explains what the conference sessions offer, lists the speakers with their titles, and gives telephone and Web site numbers for program and registration information.

Promises, promises. Forget them in advertising because there are consumer protection laws that make deceptive or misleading advertisements illegal. However, there are no such laws to protect your "consumer"—a potential employer—from deceptive or misleading information about your training, experience, abilities, or anything else you tell about yourself. The consequences of doing so can be far greater for you, though, than for an advertiser. If and when that employer detects the deception, your credibility is damaged not only for this job application, but for any hoped-for referrals to others.

## BRAGGING RIGHTS ARE DIFFERENT FROM TRUTH STRETCHERS

Salespeople know that when their product receives an award or is paid a compliment, they can use it successfully. The same works in advertising and in your application of advertising principles to your break-in plans.

When Volkswagen introduced its "New Beetle" in 1998 it didn't need to stretch the truth. The problem for the advertiser was to even approach the effectiveness of the campaign for the original version of the Volkswagen Beetle, which sold in the United States from 1949 to 1979. It was widely considered to be the best campaign ever created for a consumer product. VW hopes to cash in on that original campaign and renew the public's feelings of goodwill for the product with such headlines as "Is it possible to go backwards and forwards at the same time?" And "A car like this comes along only twice in a lifetime."

Instead of making unmerited claims, the original campaign used slogans such as "Think small" to turn the Beetle's disadvantages into selling points. The new campaign, instead of falsely implying it is a fast car, speaks to its "underpower": The headline asks "0–60?" then replies, "Yes." As the *New York Times* states, "Those ads were instrumental in transforming a tiny, tinny car into a symbol of freedom and nonconformity—and thereby revolutionized the way Americans buy automobiles by abandoning hollow boasts of status and size in favor of low-key, intelligent pitching." Another point is that people pay attention to what other people think and say about something they're interested in. Testimonials and endorsements are strong influencers in advertising. Gather them to use for your upcoming presentation. (More about the use of testimonials in Chapter 5.)

## Writing Advertising Messages

Selling is at the heart of an advertising message. It's persuasion—persuading someone to buy something, to believe something, to do something.

Regardless of the medium and the differences of format for each medium, the heart of the advertising message is basically the same.

## There's Always a Headline. It Captures the Attention.

Every ad has a headline. It's the first thing a person sees, reads, or hears, and it can be the difference between success and failure.

Robert W. Bly, in his book *The Copywriter's Handbook* (Henry Holt and Company, 1990), explains what the headline is as it appears in a variety of media:

In a print advertisement, it is the headline and the visual.

In a brochure, it's the cover.

In a radio or TV commercial, it's the first few seconds of the commercial.

In a direct-mail package, it's the copy on the outer envelope or the first few sentences in the letter.

In a sales presentation, it's the first few slides or flip charts.

"No matter how persuasive your body copy or how great your product, your ad cannot sell if it does not attract your customer's attention," says Bly. And that's the purpose of a headline.

Adman David Ogilvy explains it as the "telegram" that helps the reader decide whether or not to read the copy.

"On average," he says, "five times as many people read the headline as read the body copy. When you have written your headline, you have spent 80 cents out of your dollar." That means four out of five readers read the headline and skip the rest of the ad.

So what should a headline do? First, it must get attention. If it doesn't do that, there went your entire dollar.

Then it should zero in on the target audience. Finally, it should nudge—no, shove—the reader into the body copy.

## The "Grabber Graf"

Every ad begins with a "grabber graf." This should be true for every piece of writing, whether it's a print ad, any kind of broadcast or electronic ad, or a letter or presentation package. If the first line of the first paragraph doesn't grab the reader's attention and interest, the rest of the message is dead.

So how do you grab your prospects' attention? Move around to the other side of the table and sit in that chair for awhile. Get inside your prospective customers' heads. Think like they do. (We'll walk you through this process in Chapter 6: Know the Customer.)

## Give 'Em the Facts

You've gathered the facts—the selling features—you want these potential customers to know. But facts are a bit bony. You'll need to put some flesh on them.

William Safire, writing in the *New York Times*, notes that "Nobody talks in paragraphs." We want our writing to be a substitute for a friendly chat, so write like you talk.

The conversational style is especially important in advertising. It makes for easier reading, and the reader is more inclined to think of the advertiser as a friend. Someone he or she can trust. Pompous writing is boring, and no one has the time or energy to plow through that kind of a message no matter how much he or she might want or need what you're offering.

One way to achieve this conversational tone is to break a lot of the writing rules you grew up with:

- End a sentence with a preposition. Example: That's the kind of ad agency I want to work for.
- Use sentence fragments. This book is full of them. Example, in a graf above: "more inclined to think of the advertiser as a friend. Someone he or she can trust."
- Begin a few sentences with conjunctions. Again, this book is full of them. Example: beginning a sentence with *and*

or *but* reads much more like we speak. And it helps keep a sentence from lengthening out into a paragraph.

- Occasional one-sentence grafs are a plus. Why do you think the *New York Times* was called "the gray lady" for so many of the years before, and even after, any newspaper used color? Because of the long, gray blocks of type. One-sentence grafs can break up that gray look.
- Organize those selling points. Each ad should have a primary selling point, and the headline should shout it. But undoubtedly there are important secondary points that expand on the main selling point. These secondary points must be covered *in the order of their importance* in the body copy.

## Ask for the Order

The close to the advertising message is meant to make the reader take action. If the message is about a product or service, it's probably a request for an order. No salesperson would walk away after making a sales pitch without asking for an order. That's wasted time, effort, and, in ads, a waste of space and money.

Often it takes a bit of thinking about just what response you want readers to make. Do you want them to send for more information, such as a brochure, booklet, or free literature? Or do you want them to place an order? That may call for some comparisons between your product and that of the competition. And it certainly calls for stimulating immediate action because, if interest lags, it may completely die when an ad is set aside with intentions of responding later.

## MAKE FUN OF ADVERTISING

Whether you boast an advertising or marketing degree or just like the thought of working in the advertising field, take what you know and run with it. Have fun! And when you're ready to write your query letters and presentation copy, don't forget to give it some snap and some pop. Forget the crackle, though.

There's much more to advertising than appears here. You'll get a lot more about the basics in Section II: Using the Principles of Good Advertising to Develop Your "Break-in" Plan.

## LET'S TALK ABOUT BRANDING

A headline over the advertising column in the *New York Times* reads "National Advertisers Strive to Brand Their Product Names on the Minds of the Consumer." A part of your challenge is to brand *your* name on the mind of your target audience.

No company could do a better job of branding than Hallmark Cards, Inc. Yet they're still not satisfied. "Hallmark is working to move from being a brand consumers prefer to a brand consumers insist on," Irvine O. Hockaday Jr., president and chief executive of the company, told those attending the eighty-eighth annual conference of the Association of National Advertisers. Obviously, they've built customer trust to an economic advantage. You must build it into a career advantage.

## THEN THERE'S CYBER ADVERTISING

It may feel as if this whole break-in process is like getting around on training wheels. Well, if you're not up to speed about new-tech advertising, you'll be as limited as a toddler without any form of transport.

If you're not setting your "site" on the future, you'll be as obsolete as the word "dial" is in switching TV stations.

With the growing importance of cyberspace advertising, at least a speaking acquaintance with the medium is essential. Because online work is leaving agency media departments and going to specialists, you may need only that speaking acquaintance. Web ads, e-mail (which has become direct mail without the postage stamp), fax advertising, and other interactive types of advertising are discussed in Chapter 11.

It's a fact: The winds of change are blowing mighty strong. If you aren't with it, you'll get blown aside.

# chapter 3

## Three Routes to Get You There

For many people, one of the great enticements to follow a career in advertising is that it's never humdrum. There is constant change. There's a constant flow of new opportunities, new problems, new avenues of communication, along with the challenges of taking the explosion of new-tech tools and making them work for the client.

There are many divisions of advertising and many, many ways to advertise. That means there's a range of jobs in the ad business that makes it possible for just about anyone to find stimulating, enjoyable, productive work no matter what one's personality or aptitude. You not only have to know what that range is, but how and where you'll find the best fit for your temperament and abilities.

It's essential, before you decide what job type to go after, to thoroughly "know the product"—you—which you'll assess in Chapter 5. But before you make any decisions, to have the greatest advantage it helps to know the three routes that can get you to your desired destination.

That's what this chapter is all about: the three superhighways that will get you to your roughly mapped-out destination:

- Tie up with an agency
- Join a company's in-house advertising department
- Freelance or join a support resource group

(There are a number of side roads and backcountry byways for each route. They may not get you there quite as quickly, but they will give you a look at the scenery along the way. They are, however, where you may find a previously unthought-of, highly interesting place that better suits your needs and your temperament.)

## ROUTE 1—THE CONVENTIONAL AGENCY

There are some 5,000 advertising agencies, ranging in size from two or three individuals, one of whom undoubtedly is the owner and with annual billings well under $1 million, to agencies with branches around the world, thousands of employees, and billings in the billions of dollars. Not bad as a break-in field when you consider that would-be journalists have a pool of only 1,520 daily newspapers.

Just as metropolitan daily newspapers offer a wider range of services than small-town weeklies, larger agencies tend to offer a wider range of services than smaller agencies—from print ads and broadcast commercials to market research and accounting, even to public relations and publicity in some cases. There also are what in the industry are considered midsize agencies, which employ 600 people or more.

Then there are smaller agencies. No one seems willing to define "smaller" in this case, but if you have a choice when you're beginning your career, pick a smaller agency. There you have more opportunities to be involved. Clients' budgets are smaller, so the challenges may be far greater, but the range in the work you do will be broader—and the satisfaction when the clients' goals are achieved is vastly greater.

### Agency Consolidation Is Rampant

Even though a few advertising agencies are expanding into megamarketing bureaus with services ranging from direct marketing to public relations, many others are going in exactly the opposite direction. The downsizing bug that has bitten so many corporations of every type has also done a bit of biting in the ad agency business. This new trend is a preference to close down various in-agency departments and to contract with a myriad of support services on a per-project basis. For many agencies this has proven to be beneficial not only financially but also because they no longer are limited to the extent of the abilities and talents of their own people. Hiring freelancers or outside service groups often gives them more depth and breadth in the scope of services they can offer. The executive vice president and account services director at an agency that traces its roots back to 1916, told a reporter from the *New York Times*, "At the heart of what we do is anticipating clients' needs, and clients' needs are changing. It became obvious we needed greater depth of resources to bring us to the next level."

When *Advertising Age* did its annual survey for 1997 covering employment at the top thirty agencies, they found that "Employment swings [among] the top thirty group is decidedly mixed." Some New York–based shops have seen staffing numbers rise, while others have experienced huge drop-offs. A strong trend toward mergers and acquisitions plays a major part in these employment swings.

The industry publication also found that "instead of adding new staff at the core level—the traditional ad agency stripped of its specialty add-ons and independent operating units—are beefing up employment on their consolidated side, some of this fed by acquisitions in high-growth ad specialties." Later, in the third section of this chapter about support resource groups, you'll hear from Ray Champney, an international advertising agency president, who tells how his agency has moved to consolidate, what his agency looks for in the resource people it calls on, and how arrangements differ.

The strategy works for even the smallest agencies. They, too, have been able to expand their services from merely providing layout and design for print ads to providing just about anything a client needs or wants.

## Agency Operations

Even though many of the traditional agency operations may be assigned outside the agency these days, let's look at these operations as if they were all still under one roof as a way to better understand what departments and types of personnel are needed in each department and what departments make up a full-service agency.

## Management

Every business, every branch office, and every department of a company has someone in charge. So it is with an ad agency. Those in charge are the ones who set policies, carry out, or see that policies set by those higher up are carried out. If they're department heads, they answer to the president, CEO, or COO. If they're top executives, they answer to stockholders or whoever owns the agency. Under management fall the various departments within an agency, which include:

Account management and account executives
Creative services
Traffic control
Production
Media analysis and buying
Research
Accounting
Legal

Within each broad division there are often specific categories. For example, creative services includes writers, artists, TV and radio producers, and print producers. Individual jobs will be explored and explained in Chapter 4.

## Types of Agencies

Many agencies have a mix of clients; others specialize. For example, there are those that handle only *business-to-business accounts*, which means their advertising focuses on products and services that are used by businesses, so the ads appear primarily in trade publications.

Another type is the agency that serves banks, brokerage houses, and investment services. They're tabbed *financial agencies*. *Travel agencies* specialize in working for hotels and tourist organizations. There are health-care and medical agencies. The latter represent only medical and pharmaceutical products, with advertising directed mainly to professionals in the medical field. And of course there are *entertainment advertising agencies* that focus on theater, motion picture, and other forms of entertainment products.

A couple of examples of specialty agencies: Deb Gugel's Dallas-based, twenty-three-employee agency caters to restaurants and retailers that produce their ads in-house or have creative work done by boutiques with no media-buying capabilities. A much larger group, Select Communications, with offices in New York, Paris, and two cities in Germany, specializes in fashion and fragrance brands.

## If You Decide to Go the Agency Route

Even though agencies of all sizes have set a practice of downsizing, it's the smaller ones you should look to first when you begin your job search. Why? Because they have smaller staffs they can offer a wider diversification of work. Not only will you be able to perform in a variety of areas to see how you actually fit, you'll also have an opportunity for training you'll rarely find in large agencies.

Check The Agency Red Book, *Standard Directory of Advertising Agencies*, which lists agencies and their clients, to get an idea of the degree of specialization or diversification of each agency.

## ROUTE 2—IN-HOUSE ADVERTISING DEPARTMENT

Before you attempt to get a little exercise by jumping to conclusions, know this. Just because a corporation has an advertising department doesn't mean it does its own advertising.

Some corporations literally *do* have in-house agencies. But others may function only to direct an out-of-house agency. These are two distinctly different operations. The in-house department may perform all or only some of an agency's role. The big difference is that a company's in-house operation represents only one client—the company itself. The major benefit is that those performing on behalf of the company are totally familiar with the business and its products or services. Having a closer control over costs is another plus.

In some companies, the advertising department may design and create all of the company's advertising, which then must be presented to top management for approval. More often in today's climate, in-house operations rely on freelancers or support resource groups for their art, copy, design, and production work. This method allows the company to retain total control.

In other companies, the department is responsible for directing the work of the agency or agencies with which the company has contracted. In this case, responsibilities include ensuring that the work the agency does meets previously charted goals and reflects the company's desired image. Also, it must be sure that media buys are handled to produce the greatest returns within a predetermined budget.

An in-house operation is usually operated by an advertising director and one or two assistants. The head of a megacorporation's advertising operation may be much grander, headed by a vice president of advertising, and include separate advertising units.

## Should Company Advertising Be an Inside Job?

There are many who believe the old saying, "The doctor who treats himself has a fool for a patient." Not unexpectedly, advertising agencies stand strongest in the belief that advertising should not be done by companies for their own products or services.

Beth Miller, writing in *Advertising Age*, maintains that the old ad formulas must give way to new approaches that are more tailored to consumer needs. She gives an example of pharmaceutical companies handling their own advertising and, by her measure, thereby becoming their "own worst enemies."

Too often pharmaceutical companies are inclined to "play creative," rewriting headlines and tampering with layouts. In a perfect world, the review process should be a healthy partnership between the internal committee, the brand group, and the advertising agency, with all parties using consumer research to objectively evaluate ad effectiveness.

For the person considering this area of the advertising business there are definite pluses and minuses. The biggest plus, and the reason so many agency account service people join a corporate operation, is that they want to play a greater part in the advertising program and believe they can have a greater influence in making the corporation's advertising work.

A difficulty in following this route is that, if the function is primarily to direct an out-of-house agency, the corporate representative must have extensive knowledge of the advertising business and how it works. This usually means the person must have previously worked in a full-service agency, in a number of capacities.

## Just Out of College? Try Another Road!

Yes, there are entry-level jobs within corporate advertising departments, but as a rule it's much more difficult to get aboard right out of college, particularly if the department's function is to oversee a contracted agency's work. That's because the role calls for a broad understanding of all that an advertising program entails as well as specific knowledge of the technical aspects of advertising. Corporate advertising requires a basic understanding of how to develop goals and objectives for the overall program as well as for each project. Equally important is to know the essentials of production, media planning, research, and traffic.

## Take a Back Road to Get There

Unless you're a seasoned advertising professional, the best way to break into a corporate advertising department is to break into another area of the company. Do what an agency would do when it bids for a contract: learn everything possible about the client—in this case, the corporation. Settle in and get to know its products or services, its business practices, marketing approaches, the image it wishes to project, its clients, and its distribution channels. And *get to know the people in the advertising department*. As an insider, you will be in the best position to do all this and later to convince the powers upstairs that you're their best prospect for being hired in the advertising department.

## Does Your Personality Fit the Corporate Attitude?

There are well-known differences in temperament between agency and in-house operations. Agencies are known to be casual and laid-back. Corporations, no matter what the area, are far more structured and more formal. Are you and your personality ready to deal with a heavily administrative way of doing business? With ongoing reports and evaluations? With rigid oversight?

On the plus side, the pay in a corporation usually is much better. Job security is greater compared to job certainty with an agency; the client turnover rate among agencies is about as great as it gets, which causes immediate layoffs, a major consideration for many people. Beyond this, there is greater control of programs: the agency answers to you. And there's much less concern about client approval of your suggestions and recommendations, because you've worked from the birth of an idea to its development according to "the client's" requirements and objectives.

## You Can Take Two Roads

Once you've joined either an agency or a corporate in-house operation, there are neither rules nor obstructions to moving back and forth between the two. And the ability to understand the way both operate—and think—is priceless. Both sides often are delighted to find someone who has taken the other road, and for the special training and experience acquired while on the other route. This, of course, gives you extended options if or when layoffs happen at either site.

## ROUTE 3—SUPPORT RESOURCES—IT'S CALLED FREELANCING

Associated Press called the number of people freelancing the most monumental demographic shift since the beginning of the industrial revolution. "It also has been described," reports AP, "as a home-grown rebellion, an effort to reclaim lives and a reflection of the new age of communications and technology."

By the end of 1997, more than 40 million people worked full- or part-time for themselves or employers, temporarily or permanently, profitably or unprofitably. "A few especially cynical critics see [it] as a return to the cottage industry society of 150 years ago."

Although the figures are for all persons and all types of occupations, the condition does pertain to advertising. In other words, never has there been more opportunity than now for freelancers' goods and services.

## Independent's Day

Being independent. It's called the '90s thing to do, at least by those who have been laid off because of the prevalence of downsizing. And once they've experienced the "freedom" of being independent, it seems to be the *only* thing to do. Although there are some in the advertising business who say the consolidation phenomenon seems to have reached its peak, others strongly believe the experience has taught agencies and corporate ad departments that it's better to cut back to a skeleton crew and turn to support services when needed. In some areas, such as television commercial production, freelance producers have long been preferred because of the wider diversity they offer compared to the resources available within an agency's ranks.

The *Wall Street Journal* tells what happened to a "freelance" attorney who had previously spent time digging up evidence against plaintiffs in malpractice suits. Now, says the *Journal*, he's an advertising account planner, "one of the quirkiest and fastest-growing jobs in advertising." It's a job that attempts to "unlock consumers' hidden 'emotional' connections to products like wine, cameras, or computers and then help creative types incorporate those findings into ads."

## "Wider Is Better"

The race to downsize in ad agencies isn't just a trend. It isn't likely to change in the future, because they've learned that, as the Pontiac commercial says, "Wider is better!" A wider range of talent is more productive because it lets advertising departments and agencies maintain a skeleton staff and bring in specialists as needed. Agencies have learned that the advantage of using professional part-timers means that when the assignment is finished, the cost ceases: There's no outplacement cost and no unemployment cost.

*Brandweek* explains the trend this way: "Companies may initially turn to temporary marketers to ease a staffing emergency, but many are happy enough with their initial experience that they are employing temporary marketing professionals on a permanent part-time basis. Small companies are often drawn to temporary marketers this way, because it gives them cost-effective expertise." From this trend has come specialty temp agencies, and for employers, access to specialists through a temp agency is a big plus. There's a fast turnaround time, prescreening of candidates, and best of all, the agencies are able to match specific needs with specific expertise. Back when the need arose in the early 1990s it was difficult to find these specialists even though their numbers were growing by the day and week. There were no temp agencies that "stocked" these kinds of experienced personnel. But as always, when a need arises, there are people there with a solution—in this case, organizations that specialize in placing seasoned advertising and marketing people on a temporary basis. These pioneers have found no shortage of supply, and demand has continued to increase. As Kay Gurtin, who spotted the need and cofounded Executive Options, told *Brandweek*, "(companies) had cut tons of professionals, but they hadn't cut the work that needed to get done."

## Pluses and Minuses

As a freelancer, you're the authority. You must know the job. Beyond having the know-how, freelancing calls for the ability to perform the assigned task speedily. And there are no regular paychecks. But even more troubling is that clients sometimes take awhile to pay your billings. That calls for cash reserves.

On the other side of the coin, however, if you develop a good reputation, conduct an ongoing market-yourself campaign, and build your client list to a point where you receive sufficient assignments, there's excellent potential for bigger money than as a full-time agency employee.

Freelancing seldom is done successfully by those in the breaking-in stage of employment. It's a great first step in self-employment, especially for those with creative talents who look forward to starting their own specialty resource group. But if the step is taken before acquiring sufficient experience, competence, and expertise not only in your field but in your knowledge of how and where to market yourself, it's a real gamble.

Marilyn Bagel calls it "The First Commandment of Freelancing—Thou shalt have amassed a strong portfolio of thy work." And Bagel, who is an author, magazine writer, and an advertising copywriter, knows whereof she speaks. "You're always 'auditioning' for assignments," she says. Your portfolio, your book, your examples of your expertise are indispensable. It's obvious: freelancers are hired for their proven know-how and their ability to deliver. Even fully staffed agencies call on freelancers when there's more work than their regular staff can handle. In every case, the freelancer is expected to jump aboard as the vehicle speeds by, with no slow-downs or stops to show him or her how to do the job.

*The following advice comes from Ray Champney, an advertising pro who's been there, done that, and not only understands the best ways to do it, but the best ways to get it done.*

With more than twenty-five years working at international and domestic agencies and as president of RJC International, I have seen the connotation of "freelance" go from someone without a steady job to a valuable resource in today's business environment. Let's look at freelance from the perspective of agency management and then touch upon how one becomes a freelancer.

The term "freelance" casts a wide net when used in relation to advertising. Everything from copy to design to art direction, promotion, or even trade show management can be freelanced.

Perhaps it is best to define what freelance means as a resource to an advertising agency. Freelancers are the cadre of support troops that are in reserve and can be called upon to fill the breach when additional specialized help is needed.

It is important to remember that even within a given category of a freelance speciality, subspecialties exist. For instance, copywriters will have strengths and weaknesses relative to a business category. A travel writer will have a certain style and flair as opposed to a consumer products writer who specializes in food, or a writer who is more in tune with the new technology of today's consumer products.

This simply means that the nature of the *agency* will determine the type of freelance roster that best suits the agency's needs. A business-to-business agency will have different requirements than an agency specializing in packaged-goods clients or medical products.

In some instances a copywriter will have multiple capabilities and serve the agency well in a variety of business categories. This general overview of the considerations that come into play in establishing a roster of freelance specialists applies to all categories of freelance. The ideal situation is for an agency to have available a group of freelancers with multiple talents in several business categories served by the agency.

Let's assume that the homework has been done and several candidates have been identified as qualified freelance resources based on past experience and demonstrable work produced. They now have to fit into the operating style of the agency. More important, the freelance professional needs to understand the client's likes and dislikes in relation to style and tonality. This does not mean that writing copy or preparing layouts are dictated by the client. It means being aware of the positives and negatives, the hot buttons and turn-offs that are the idiosyncrasies of the agency's client.

You will notice that the emphasis up to this point has been on copy or layout. However, the procedure for any freelance resource will require due diligence on the part of agency management in order to select the best candidate to complement the freelance roster. By this I do not mean an elaborate process, but simply taking time to analyze agency needs in relation to talent requirements and types of personalities that will fit best.

Another factor to take into account is individual creative and work performance style as it relates to the agency or client to be served by the freelance talent. The reason I say this is that some clients require more detail than others, and it is important for a freelancer to understand and have the capability of providing the necessary back-up and detail that will make the job easier when making recommendations to the client.

For example, a client may require several different visual or copy treatments. Or, if a graphics/printing broker or production manager is the area of freelance, multiple bids from printing sources as well as several types of paper samples may be required.

These are not questions that most freelancers will ask or necessarily think about, and it is important to convey that this kind of support information is a requirement and a necessity to satisfy the agency that the freelancer can accommodate the need.

Now, let's look at how one identifies a qualified freelancer, designer, art director, copywriter, graphics production provider, printing broker, direct mail specialist, Web master, or any number of other freelance categories that apply to the creation of successful marketing and advertising programs. As with any other provider, credentials and capabilities are key factors in demonstrating the ability to perform the required freelance task. Years ago there was a TV series called *Dragnet,* and the main character, Joe Friday, was only interested in the facts. "Just the facts ma'am." This is the requirement necessary to determine the ability of an individual being considered as a candidate for a freelance assignment. Tell me and show me what you have done—either actual work produced or qualifications based on training that will be persuasive enough to demonstrate an ability to do the job.

Now that we have addressed what agency management will be looking for in a freelance specialist, it is incumbent on freelancers to prepare themselves, taking into account likely areas that will be explored as part of the assignment process.

One way to do this is to segment credentials into two separate leave-behind documents. Both of these should be brief but meaningful. The first establishes education and work experience, along with particular skills relative to the performance of the area of expertise of the freelancer. This enables one to speak in broad general terms on capabilities without focusing on a specific business category.

The complementary document will focus on business categories in which actual work has been performed. This enables the freelancer to address the category and, while doing so, to demonstrate work that has been completed for other clients. If the freelancer is light on actual experience, the first document permits the freelancer to put the best foot forward, based on effort and desire, which can be enough to get you in the door.

As you can imagine, compensation varies with experience and performance. There is no set formula or guideline, but hourly ranges can be obtained for various functions from trade publications available by subscription or at the library. My preference is to establish a flat project cost, based on the work to be performed. This simplifies the record-keeping process as well as overall project estimating on a given job. Naturally, if a project changes from the estimate, based on an assignment criterion, the estimate should be adjusted to meet the changes.

Other options, such as a commission arrangement or retainer, are possibilities for a freelancer, depending on the nature of the work.

The creativity that very often is part of what a freelancer brings to a client should be utilized by the freelancer to find assignments and structure the compensation arrangements.

Agencies are a natural source of assignments for freelancers. A consistent reminder to the decision maker is essential in order to stay top-of-mind as a potential resource.

Always try to arrange a one-on-one meeting and then follow up with the decision maker on regular intervals. How you do this is up to you—snail-mail, e-mail, telephone, or create your own follow-up system.

One trait that any freelancer must be able to demonstrate is reliability. This is a deadline business, and on-time performance is critical. As a freelancer it is essential to leave the impression that you are dependable and will deliver the assignment on time. With today's technology the ability to perform off-site and deliver the product on-site within minutes makes the freelancer a virtual asset—without the employee overhead. Conversely, a talented freelancer can reap greater rewards by not being an employee. An effective follow-up system that uses technology clearly demonstrates a freelancer's capability to follow up and follow through.

Another source of direct client freelance business can be new company start-ups or growth of existing companies. This is all public information available through local newspapers, Chamber of Commerce rosters, and public records.

The point in being a freelancer means being a businessperson first and foremost in order to sell your freelance talent.

*Raymond J. Champney is founder and president of RJC International, located in Irving, Texas.*

## What Freelance Work Is Like

Author Bradley J. Morgan describes it graphically: "Freelancers are like firemen. When the phone rings, they're ready to jump into action." Then he says, as Ray Champney does (see box), that one of the most important qualities of a good freelancer is *reliability*.

You have to know what you're doing, but you also have to act *immediately*. As Morgan says in his book *Advertising Career Directory: A Practical, One-Stop Guide to Getting a Job in Advertising* (Gale Research, 1993), even if the "account executive sat on the assignment an extra few days, or maybe the client has made some unrealistic demands . . . regardless, the deadline is the bottom line. Miss one, and you won't get a second chance."

Of course, on-their-own-ers must have connections and keep in constant contact with them to be successful as freelancers.

There's another attraction that's impossible to find in an agency or an in-house department—if you're lucky enough to become a member of a core group of freelancers who specialize in, say, media buying or copy writing, you'll be able to cash in on the group's recognition and reputation. And if it's a group in the area where you live, you can end up doing work for agencies or companies that may be hundreds, even thousands, of miles away.

So what are the prospects that down the years the need will be sufficient to warrant taking this route? Andrea Meltzer, co-owner of Executive Options, says "Companies are becoming so project-oriented that I see more and more growth coming."

## For Many, Temping Is a Lifetime Choice

If a person has the required skills, freelancing, also known as temping, may be the right route to follow. Explore your own employment desires. "The vast majority of people in professional temporary jobs are looking out of choice, either because they have family responsibilities or other interests and commitments," says Diane Charness, president of Part-Time Professional Placements.

## THE LESS TRAVELED FOURTH ROUTE

Actually, this isn't a *route*. It's more like borrowing a training video that gives you a sneak peek at the countryside you want to travel, teaches you how to operate the car, and maybe even pays you for taking the trip—before you set out on any of the three roads we've talked about. You might explain it as a shortcut that can get you to any of the three major highways.

We're talking about internships and on-the-job training (OJT). Either OJT or an internship gets more than a foot in the door. Either can become that all-important eye-stopping first paragraph on your resume that will undoubtedly get you that coveted interview. Perhaps equally important, either an internship or OJT gives you a first-person, insider's look to help you figure out if you really do want to make this business your career. And you also may be introduced to areas you'd never considered before. Plus, you may even get paid—and that's almost as good as getting paid to go to college.

The problem? They're hard to find. Supply and demand don't match up.

## Internships and OJT Have Been Downsized Too

Unfortunately, with all the mergers and consolidation going on, and with the magnifying glass focused solely on the bottom line, most internships and on-the-job training positions have been considered expendable. Some agencies, however, now recognize the benefits each provided them and are putting them back in place. For them it's a highly useful way to recruit people—particularly in the fields where it's becoming harder and harder to find trained people—and it's an opportunity for the agency to look them over before signing them on a permanent basis. Also, it's often a way to hire someone for less money than an established professional, who they can then teach to work *their* way.

For you, it probably means a hard search. Don't give up, though. It's worth all the effort you put into it. Then it means coming up with a presentation that will convince those offering the opportunity that you're the one for them. How to put it all together is covered in Chapter 9.

## About Internships

Beyond the advantages previously mentioned, an internship gives you a running start on the competition. It gives you training you'll *never* get at a college or university, no matter how close to the business the instructors are. It gives you a foot in the door with the agency or corporation offering the internship. And if they don't hire you on a permanent basis, recommendations about other places to search, and perhaps some important letters of recommendation or testimonials, could come from the contact.

It's good for the agency, too. It's the only way they can actually see what you're all about beyond the interview, to see if you're the talented, hard-working, capable, and intelligent person they want and need.

Where do you find internships? Check with your college instructors and with the career development center for information. Or check industry directories that list advertising agencies across the country. Don't be hesitant to call agencies to ask about their intern program and to talk to their intern contact.

## About On-the-Job Training

An OJT trainee is a member of the firm, albeit a new member, and a beginner in the business. All the blessings of an internship are there for the OJT-er—to be used when you're ready to move on.

It can provide that all-important first paragraph on your resume, but it also gives you the chance to look at the business from the inside out—and for the employer to see your value to the company.

An on-the-job trainee may start in any department and be systematically moved from department to department in order to become acquainted with the various agency functions. Some agencies today start their beginners in the mailroom or as administrative assistants. But the most likely places to start are media, research, traffic, or production.

Ask yourself some questions to be sure the effort it will take is worth the trouble. Ask: Is the money you'd be paid the reason you want the assignment? Do you want it in order to gain the experience that will open the doors that otherwise might be locked? If your answer is the money, forget it. It won't pay you enough to make it worth your while. If your answer is to have a look around to help you decide if this is the place for you, if it's to gain experience, and then to use that experience to open doors, then no matter how much effort is required, it will be worth it.

## THERE'S ANOTHER ROUTE

Another way into the field is to be hired as a trainee by one of the mega–mass-marketers. William Pattis suggests the best opportunities are offered with food producers such as Procter & Gamble, General Mills, and Kellogg. The advantage to these industries, says Pattis, is that the individual learns about the actual movement of goods from a client's point of view. "By working within commercial and industrial businesses, one can learn about the effects of an advertising campaign on the movement and profitability of goods over a long period of time."

## SCUTTLEBUTT ABOUT THE FUTURE

Every time you pick up a trade paper, it seems there's a story about this agency reorganizing, or that one reinventing itself, and occasionally about one that has just closed its doors.

What's the future for the agency business? The answers are as diverse as the business itself. As Howard Steinberg, president of Source Marketing, sees it, each agency seems to have a different view of the future. "While McCann bundles services to offer clients a worldwide menu of tools, Burnett appears to be unbundling to foster creative focus. The agency of the future will not be an advertising agency but a marketing agency," he says in a bylined article in *Advertising Age*.

Steinberg also predicts that "marketing campaigns—not advertising campaigns—are going to emerge that include something for every link in the distribution chain."

This is showing up in a new trend that is widespread. It's sometimes called "below-the-line." It provides services aside from general advertising, including direct marketing, media planning and buying, public relations, and just about anything else it takes to get a product or service on the market, get it recognized, and make it profitable. It's expected by some that by the year 2000 this trend will account for at least 20 percent of an agency's revenue. But then Jeffrey J. Hicks, president of Crispin Porter & Bogusky, also writing in *Advertising Age*, says "Advertisers today don't seem to want much of what traditional full-service agencies are selling. Why should great marketing minds go to work at an ad agency when all the key decisions are now being made at the companies?"

Then Hicks asks—and answers—the big question: "So what will the implications of these trends be? In the future, breakthrough creative that can run in any medium will be the most valuable and differentiated service agencies provide. Smaller agencies will be able to compete on a more even level with larger agencies as the economics of scope associated with the traditional full-service structure disappear."

The only advice that makes any sense is—stay tuned. Times, they are a changin' on a daily basis! The best way to stay on top of industry trends is to keep up with the industry "trades," such as *Advertising Age*, and by faithfully reading the business pages of the *New York Times* and the *Wall Street Journal*. In any case, keep your eyes and ears open and absorb all you can.

# chapter 4

## Kinds of Jobs in Advertising

There are basically two types of jobs in advertising—right-brained and left-brained work.

If you're so right-brained you tilt when you walk, knowing which way to go is easy. You'll do best and be happiest in one of the areas tabbed "creative." If your left brain pretty much rules your thinking, head for one of the more structured types of work such as research, media, business affairs, accounting, or traffic.

Of course, we're not all strictly one type or the other. Most of us have a good mix of right- and left-brain functioning, which means we can look into joining *any* of the areas that fascinate us, that we have a passion for. (There's that word again—passion!)

In fact, a growing body of recent research has turned up new data that almost guarantees everyone has perhaps previously unrecognized creative abilities. R. J. Whittier of Third Age News Service "suggests that enormous powers of creativity can flourish in 'ordinary' people . . . that many can tap creative reserves to become more effective on the job or to find outlets of their own expression."

Wherever you head within the advertising business, there is one ability that you must have. You must be able to *adapt*—to hectic schedules, to working with or within a group, to pressures to produce, and to little or no working privacy. The good part is that almost everyone can adapt *if they want to!* The trouble is, many people think that what they must have is what they've always had, and therefore changes are insurmountable.

So, before you take off running on a road you're not yet sure heads where you want to go, let's line up a list of jobs within the two categories. And we'll take a closer look at the posts within the individual divisions.

## THERE ARE ROUGHLY TWO DIVISIONS—PLUS A THIRD!

"Creative" is the all-encompassing, self-explanatory term that covers writing, designing, casting, art, and graphics.

Then there's the other division that includes researchers and project directors; media buying, planning and supervision; traffic, coordinating, supervising; financial management and accounting; production; account services and supervision; and business affairs. Some agencies also have legal departments.

The third isn't really a division, because these people work both sides of the fence. They're what are called office management and support people. The category of office management obviously includes top-level managers, office managers, and their assistants, but it also includes librarians and information specialists. Support people operate the mailroom; they're also messengers, reception-ists, assistants, and typists.

Then there is a totally new type of specialist being sought these days, who may fall into any of the three categories. This work calls for training and experience beyond left- or right-brain tendencies. These specialists are known as cyber-brains, whose cyber-savvy can mean the difference in the entry-level salaries in other areas of $25,000 to $30,000, to $40,000 to $65,000 to do Net work. To get a perspective on this area, read Chapter 11: *Reaching Out to New-Tech Advertising*.

Now let's look at what each job entails within each division.

## Right-Brained People Take Note

The first kind of job that comes to mind for a number of people wanting to break into advertising falls under the broad term of "creative."

Creative is alluring. It's where the participants can see results of their work show up on the pages of newspapers, magazines, television screens, billboards, or wherever the client's advertising appears. This idea of being the parent of a visible, final advertising product is very seductive.

It's also a hot seat. As Peter Mayle says in *Up the Agency* (St. Martin's Press, 1995), most creative departments "have their share of nonconformists and anarchists, and it requires the combined talents of a wet nurse and a prison warden to deal with them." It's certainly not your everyday 9-to-5 corporate job.

The range within each area of creative is broad. At the top there may be a creative director, an associate creative director, and a creative supervisor. Below them, the creative is made up primarily of copywriters and artists. They're the people who create the actual advertising. They work in a variety of media—print advertising for newspapers and magazines, radio and television commercials, outdoor billboards, direct mail pieces, or whatever medium research shows is the best route to reach a client's targeted audience. The range of talents and experience required within the broad category of creative can be broad, too. For example, a person developing a TV commercial must understand the entire process of how it takes form—from initial idea, to storyboard, to selecting and casting the best talent for each commercial, to filming, to the finished product.

Years back, creatives never saw clients except perhaps to sit quietly and listen to them detail their needs. Today, though situations vary from agency to agency, most creatives present their own work to the client, describe its fit in the goal achievement strategy, justify it if necessary, and explain how and why it will work.

## Copywriting

There are many different kinds of copywriting, such as writing headlines to get attention, writing to communicate, and writing to sell. And there are different types of copywriting—scripts for TV or radio commercials, print ad copy, the super-condensed copy for outdoor boards, or whatever the ad plan calls for.

The ability to write copy that is clear, convincing, and speaks directly to the targeted group is essential. Writers must also be able to write in whatever style is demanded for each ad: formal, informal, or technical. Often it includes a catchy phrase within the copy that becomes the well-remembered slogan for a company and may even set an image for the company. It's what they say in the industry "Turns Splash Into Cash." Who can forget the Leo Burnett agency's slogan for United Airlines, developed in 1965, "Fly the friendly skies?" Or, "Nothing beats a great pair of L'Eggs," which not incidentally gets the name of the product into the catch-phrase. Or "It's right at Eckerd," with its double meaning and which also includes a reminder of the corporate name.

Copywriters don't sit down, write the copy, and then disappear into the twilight. They're part of the team that must help decide on art or graphics, and on the music and special effects if it's a commercial. They must do revises when called for and help with making changes a client may request.

There can be a senior copywriter, a copywriter, and a junior copywriter. Junior copywriter is the title usually given to entry-level writers, and in order to expand their knowledge of their work, they're usually assigned to a variety of jobs.

Good copywriters are in great demand because they have the talent to give life and memory to a product or service. But getting hired as a copywriter isn't always easy. You can come from a great school and have excellent grades, but the person doing the hiring wants to see what you can do. That means collecting examples of your work to show when you make your presentation. Start now so you'll have adequate samples and examples when you go about putting together your presentation package in Chapter 9.

## Art, Graphics, and Visuals

This is the visual side of advertising. It's the part of an ad or a TV commercial that readers and viewers see first. Art and graphics creators, like copywriters, must have special talents and abilities. (And, again like copywriters, when applying for a position, they must *show* what they can do. So keep in mind you'll need to begin your collection of examples as quickly as possible.)

These are the people who are sometimes called visualizers because they bring the message to life in the minds of viewers. They're responsible for setting the style of an ad, designing the layout, and even choosing typeface styles and sizes in order to attract and influence readers to pause and peruse the ad.

From the beginning of a project, the person developing the visuals must work closely with the assigned copywriter, or in the case of a TV commercial, with the producer. In larger agencies with full creative service departments, the art department is called "the bullpen," an expressive description of the kind of pressure and "herding" that goes on there. There may be a senior art director and an art director. Entry-level jobs may include an assistant art director or a bullpen artist.

## Left Brainers Are the Advance Crew

A huge amount of work takes place before creatives can even think about the direction in which they'll use their talents to produce an ad or commercial for a client.

Let's look at the work that most left brainers lean toward. Then we'll glance at places where a person who uses a bit of both sides of the brain can settle in and be comfortable.

### Research

Researchers probably should be first on the list. Clients rightly demand that the often large sums of money they spend on their advertising is well spent. So researchers are responsible for pinning down the identity of the audience that best fits the client's product or service and for gathering and analyzing information, including evaluating competitive media research. The data and information they dig out is at the heart of every plan and advertising strategy developed for each client.

In other words, research guides the direction a client's plan must take. It sets the focus or a theme. And it determines the types of media that will precisely target the client's designated audience. If surveys are called for, researchers are responsible for designing the questionnaires and evaluating the results.

They're also the ones who test whether the material developed within the creative departments is effective in reaching the specified audience and measuring its "reach (total impressions) and frequency (how often they are published or broadcast)." It's called "concept testing" and is the assessment of consumers' reactions. "Copy testing" may also be conducted to determine the effectiveness of the advertising and whether it is accomplishing the goals set for it.

Large agencies usually have their own in-house research department, and smaller agencies contract with independent research groups. There may be a reason for contracting outside help. The question of credibility may be raised when an agency does its own research, because the results could be slanted to the agency's favor. This may be the reason more and more researchers are calling themselves "strategic planners."

## Media

Media are the means by which an advertising message reaches a targeted group. No matter how great the message and how effective the style or format and the words or visuals, if no one sees it, it's worthless.

Selecting the media to reach a specific, targeted group is the job of the media department. Media planning and buying, along with supervision, are the principal functions of a media department. These people used to be—and sometimes still are—thought of as bookkeepers who keep files on rates, circulation, and program ratings. Or as advertising mogul Leo Burnett once described their job, "to listen patiently to competitive sales pitches by the honeybees of the advertising world and, when the time came, to wangle an ad into a far-forward position or a commercial into a better time slot."

Today, the functions they perform are different from any others within an agency, except for the research they may be required to do if there is no research department within the agency. They must know who the client's competitors are, who the purchasers—and potential purchasers—are and where they live, their interests, the publications they read and the broadcast stations they watch and listen to, and what medium—or combination of media—will reach them.

These are the people who take the researched information and devise a media plan and strategy that fits the client's advertising goals and put together a recommended schedule. They decide where advertising should be placed so that it will reach the identified target audience. They do the buying of print space and radio and television time and the haggling for better placement or a preferable time slot.

Not only agencies have media departments. There are separate, autonomous media-buying services that provide services for small agencies and sometimes even for major advertisers who prefer separate services to those of an agency. But more importantly, clients rather than agencies or independent services are more apt to handle their own media-planning and buying today than in past years.

People providing these services must be able to work well with others in the agency or service, as well as with clients. An example of their interaction is the advice they must give creatives about changes such as new print unit sizes, new advertising vehicles, and any and all new developments that may impact present in-place methods, plans, or strategies.

An entry-level position is usually as an assistant planner or junior buyer. Further up the ladder are the media supervisor, associate media director, and the media director who is in charge of the entire media services department.

In *Advertising Career Directory*, edited by Ronald W. Fry, readers are told that "the media person's contribution is more tangible, more apparent, than that of his or her colleagues. If you prefer to be a specialist rather than a generalist, find it stimulating to talk to clients about their business, and feel comfortable being regarded as an expert whose viewpoint is largely unquestioned, media may be the right place for you."

Be ready for more change, though. In August 1997 *Advertising Age* warned "every day advances the way advertising time and space are purchased. And as agencies reinvent themselves for the 21st century, there's a lot of posturing and adjusting going on . . . the face of how TV time is analyzed, digitized and amalgamated will be strikingly different the morning of January 1, 2000 than in 1997."

If you hope to break in here, start digging immediately and continue searching for the kinds of changes that are coming and what you'll need to know to keep qualified and informed.

### The Business Affairs Department

The business affairs department is another area where left brainers fit right in. Its domain is accounting and financial matters, including client fees and billings, media billings and payments, talent payments and production costs, and payroll for agency staff. There also can be investment decisions to make and actions to take, as well as long-range financial plans to construct and oversee. Even when top management handles investment buying, the business affairs department is involved.

Advertising may be one of the most creative businesses around, but without careful, constant attention to cash income and outgo the business collapses. And collapse can come in a flash if clients delay paying their bills.

The number of people in the department depends upon the size of the agency. Numbers can range from a single person to an entire group of bookkeepers and accountants under the supervision of a controller, the chief financial officer, and ultimately the treasurer.

### Traffic

The people in traffic are responsible for coordinating and scheduling all creative and production jobs. They make sure that commercials and ads get where they're supposed to be and that they're there on time.

Jan Greenberg gives an excellent description of this department in her book *Advertising Careers: How Advertising Works and the People Who Make It Happen.*

> With so much going on at once in so many different departments, it is obvious that there is a real potential

for chaos within agencies. Somebody has to be responsible for the workflow from the time the agency gets the go-ahead from the client to begin creative work until that work is completed and, in finished form, sent to the media in which it will appear. The aptly named traffic department handles this.

Former advertising executive S. William Pattis in his books about advertising likens this department to the air traffic control tower at an airport. "It is the department where timetables and deadlines that govern an agency's activities are monitored."

There's print traffic and broadcast traffic. Print traffic may be involved in production of the ad, but broadcast traffic is only in charge of distributing the finished commercial, with exact scheduling instructions and with checking that timetables are followed.

Everyone in the ad business agrees that for those who work in traffic there are a couple of very important qualifications. Being left-brained—described in the business as "detail-oriented"—is a major consideration. The second essential is an ability to get along and work with people in all departments, because the job calls for contact with almost every agency function. The payoff is that it can be a footbridge to the media or to account management departments.

## Production—Print and Broadcast

Print production is responsible for turning artwork and copy into finished ads in newspapers and magazines. Broadcast production organizes the entire TV and radio commercial operation—from casting to the final shoot, to taping, to the finished product.

Production is where the idea, the description of the idea, and approval of the idea by the client, come together and become reality. In most agencies, print and broadcast production are separate—and with good reason. The two functions are as different as, well, you fill in the cliché.

**Print Production** This is where print ads are readied for runs in print media. A layout is prepared by an artist and a copywriter for presentation to and approval by the client. In a smaller agency the layout may be done by the art director. In larger agencies, bullpen layout artists may do the work.

Once the agency has approval from the client, production steps in. Working with creative, they choose the appropriate typeface, photo, or art and prepare purchase orders. Often the people in creative make the final decisions, and that's when the production job becomes one of supervising the work, ensuring accuracy of the finished product, and being sure that each publication in which the ad will appear receives its own copy. It can be a highly technical process.

The break-in to this department can be accomplished as a proofreader or as an assistant production manager, but knowledge of and some training in typography, layout, and design are the usual requirements.

**Broadcast Production** More advertising dollars are spent on television than on any other media form. So television production is highly important. The producer doesn't stand alone. He or she is part of the team (with the copywriter and art director) who, together, produce commercials. The producer is, however, the coordinator of both people and processes, including all the creative and management facets of the project.

The producer, after handling all of the scheduling and preproduction and postproduction details and technicalities, becomes the translator of the storyboard, transforming it from a series of illustrations of the scenes in the commercial into an eye-catching, person-stopping message that accomplishes the client's goal.

This certainly is one of the most difficult jobs to land. The entry-level title with a mega-agency is assistant producer or production assistant. However, at most agencies producers don't have assistants, which means you must take a side road to get into the agency and then make yourself available to help in any way you can. Eventually, you may get that assistant's position or, after a number of years of learning and proving you know the ropes, perhaps you'll land the big job.

### Accounts Services and Supervision

Accounts services includes the position of account execs, a job you'd think would be as secure as the account itself. But as far back as 1995, *Adweek* reported that "in this era of restructuring and cost crunching, no agency species is more threatened—perhaps with extinction—than the poor, benighted account executive."

The account exec's job focuses on working with the client to conceive ways, through advertising, to increase the client's sales and to guarantee not only that the work comes in on time but on target. A big part of the job is getting along with the client and keeping the client happy and satisfied. Within the agency it calls for working with all departments—from research and media, to traffic, account planning, and especially creative.

The pressure is as high here as anywhere in the agency. Some in the business describe account execs as the client's representative at the agency. Others see them as the agency's rep to the client. So pressure comes from both sides of the fence. Not only must they "sell" the expertise and skills of the agency to the client, they must create enthusiasm for the client and the client's product or service within the agency.

This is an area that calls for a bit of a right- and left-brain mix. It calls for becoming an expert in the client's field. He or she must be an idea person who can come up with creative suggestions, while still being responsible for the work done for the client and being sure that the account turns a profit for the agency. The account exec is also responsible for managing the client's advertising budget.

The job demands strong verbal as well as writing skills. Amiable, congenial, friendly, likable, outgoing, warm—all synonyms for "personable"—are absolute requirements. Well-groomed is an outdated description for today's executives, but it's difficult to come up with a better phrase describing another requisite for the job. Brains are a necessity—not just intelligence, but creativity, imagination, and inventiveness—as is outstanding sales ability, in order to sell to both the client and to the agency's people.

Bradley J. Morgan and Joseph M. Palmisano, in *Advertising Career Directory* (Gale Research, 1993), say,

> The *great* account person considers himself a business manager. He is providing a unique service to his client. The *exceptional* account executive is fiscally responsible and responsive to his client—doing hard-bill estimates, revised estimates (when necessary), and on-time billing, with documentation for out-of-pocket expenses. These, a good financial background and understanding of agency finances, are musts for the talented, growth-motivated agency account executive.

Assistant account executive is considered the entry-level position. As S. William Pattis explains in *Careers In Advertising* (VGM Career Horizons, 1996), the position of assistant account executive usually involves a lot of paperwork and legwork. However, he says, "It is a good place to view the inner workings of the department and to learn from the more experienced account executives."

Andrew Jaffe, who wrote the 1995 *Adweek* article about the potential for extinction of AEs, acknowledges that this conjecture "may seem a fairly heretical judgment regarding what many still consider to be the Crazy Glue that binds client to agency." Jaffe also points out that in this new downsliced business world, not only this area is in danger. "Trafficking can be done by computer, account planners can write the briefs, and creative people show and sell their own work."

Even though account executives may be an endangered species at some agencies, others are considering whether to give clients *more* services. The information is passed along here so that you're aware of a seeming trend and will look hard before you leap.

### Account Planner

Don E. Schultz, author and professor at Northwestern University, explains a relatively new position at many agencies: account planner. He says the new position is having a major impact on how advertising campaigns are developed.

The account planner's assigned duty is to represent the consumer and his or her views to the advertising agency during the planning process. The account planner then helps the accounts services, creative, and media people develop advertising that will fill consumers' wants and needs for information about the product or service.

### Agency Management

The agency's chief executives are on the top rung of the agency ladder. If your goal is to one day head up an agency, don't worry now about which area of the business to break into. The ladders that took today's agency heads to the top were grounded in just about every department—creative services, account management, media, research. It's not where they started that was important to their achievement, it's that they have special leadership skills and abilities; people with these qualities can be found in many different areas.

At large agencies there may be more than one chief. The duties may be spread around among a CEO, a COO, and a CFO—together called an executive team. At smaller agencies there is generally only one or two people in charge, and they're usually the owners.

## SUPPORT PEOPLE

As mentioned at the beginning of this chapter, there are the all-important basic support people, without whom an agency does not exist. They run the mailroom and are librarians, messengers, receptionists, assistants, and typists. They handle all the housekeeping responsibilities and sometimes also handle personnel operations.

The only thing different about these positions from those in other types of businesses is the "ads-mosphere!" Most businesses are structured with a very businesslike atmosphere. But in advertising the atmosphere may be a bit more demanding, always challenging, and a lot more lively.

## ADVERTISING AND *NEW* MEDIA JOBS

You'd have to have been in hibernation for the better part of your life not to have heard about advertising on the Internet. Obviously, if there's Internet advertising there's a need for people who create it.

The need has exploded, and colleges now are turning out graduates with multimedia degrees. *Advertising Age* reports that "graduates with a master's degree in advertising and no multimedia experience earn an average of $25,000 to $30,000. With multimedia experience however, salaries increase to $40,000 to $65,000. The need is so new that it's difficult to locate schools that offer this special curriculum. So seven University of Texas [UT] students created a site that "teaches people how to effectively use advertising on Web sites."

Professor of Advertising at UT, John Lechenby, says, "Although this kind of experience doesn't guarantee that a graduate will be hired, it can't hurt. In such a changing field you have to catch as catch can, but it's great to have a foundation." The managing partner at Modem Media, an interactive agency, offers information worth heeding. "I'm looking for smart people who can think strategically and creatively. Interactive experience isn't a requirement, but it's a plus."

Chapter 11 of this book, *Reaching Out to New-Tech Advertising*, offers information about the construction of cyber ads and about this relatively new area where there also are specialty agencies called cyber-advertising agencies.

## JOBS IN CORPORATE AD DEPARTMENTS

The second of the three routes to breaking into advertising we discussed in Chapter 3 is by way of the corporate world—the in-house advertising department of a corporation. But this isn't the route to take if it's your first career step after graduation, because too much knowledge and experience are required about advertising, including how it works and how to work it.

For those with such knowledge and experience, however, the job opportunities vary as widely as the nature of the corporations.

The size of the department and the breadth of the functions it performs determine the job types.

Although the structure of a corporate advertising department is vastly different from that of an agency, they require the same types of people with the same experience and training. The principal difference, says S. William Pattis in *Careers in Advertising*, is that "people who work in these house agencies are on salary like other company employees, [so] they are less concerned with profit and loss than are the employees of independently owned agencies."

For a corporation with several different products, there may be a person assigned to each product or product group, called a brand manager, under whose direction falls advertising, sales promotion, and market and profitability research and strategy. The emphasis here is on the need for business talents rather than creative advertising abilities. Much greater importance in this position is placed on marketing, so a brand manager must know and understand three elements: marketing, advertising, and business.

Retailers almost without exception do their own advertising, in house. The need here is for the full range of the same advertising types as work in agencies, including copywriters, media, research, and traffic people, along with TV producers and art directors, depending on their target audiences. For the brand manager, time is almost always the major challenge. Producing ads or commercials, sometimes at breakneck speed, means caliber and creativity sometimes must give way to timing demands.

There is more information about jobs in corporate advertising departments in Chapter 3.

# section II

## Use the Principles of Good Advertising to Develop Your "Break-in" Plan

Getting ready for the break-in is as easy as 1-2-3. Well, actually 1-2-3-4-5-6! In this section we use six easy steps to follow the proven principles of advertising to get you where you want to go.

The six steps are the six strategies used by advertising agencies to capture clients. You can apply these same strategies to find the position you want in advertising.

1. Know the product (you)
2. Know the customer (potential employers)
3. Know the competition (who's competing for the job you want)
4. Develop a plan
5. Put together a presentation package
6. Make the presentation, pitch the "product," and capture the "account"

Throughout this section are tested and proven ground rules that work for advertising and will work for you while they also perform as an advertising refresher course. Also, keep in mind that there are no hard and fast advertising rules, or methods of how to brainstorm for ideas, how concepting and planning discussions are conducted, and how presentations are put together and presented.

# chapter 5

## Step 1—First Up Is to Know the Product

In this case, you are the product. You—the product—are the most important factor in this quest. Without you, there's no hunt, no journey. As in advertising, a total understanding of the product comes before even the simplest campaign can be developed.

Of course you also must intimately know potential consumers and identify who are your competitors. That comes later, though, after you're sure the ad business is the place you want to be, after you've figured out what area you want to break into, and that you have the characteristics to be happy there. If the "product" itself isn't right for this "market," if it doesn't have the essential ingredients or components to satisfy "buyers," they may buy it once, but not again, no matter how much or how well it's advertised.

## IS ADVERTISING THE PLACE YOU *REALLY* WANT TO BE?

Do you know enough about this sometimes wild and wacky business to know it's the place for you? To know whether you're right for it? Frankly, you may not be sure until you've done some investigating on your own or until you get inside and have firsthand knowledge about the business.

Someone—probably an ad pro—said that the only sure way to beat the competition is to stay ahead of them. That means not just knowing you want to be in advertising, but being able to specify attributes you know the consumers need and want. It also means you know and are able to spell out exactly where in the business you want to be. There are a number of fields within the field, and one may be as different from another as accounting is from dress designing.

So what's a job in advertising like, from a pro's view?

"It's work so absorbing that you'll never know what time it is," says Charlotte Beers, chairman emeritus of Ogilvy & Mather Worldwide. "It's a bit of a crazy quilt . . . compelling, absorbing, satisfying, stressful, and risky," she writes in *Advertising Age*. On the other hand, fear dominates the business, warns another professional, Judith Katz, in her book *The Ad Game* (Barnes & Noble Books). Fear of the client, fear of the supervisor, fear that you'll lose business despite . . . doing a great job for the client.

## It's a Tough, Hard, Competitive Business

Advertising is a risky and stressful business. Getting fired is about as prevalent as agencies losing clients. And just as with traditional agency reviews by clients—which Charlotte Beers calls "the Dance of Death because the win rate is about one in ten"—there are the regular reviews of those who work in the business.

Fair warning: This isn't an easy field to break into these days. Downsizing is rampant. And many agencies are closing down their in-house operations and hiring outside support services on a per-project basis. (For ways to break into support services see Chapter 3: Route 3.)

So why would anyone, knowing all these negatives, seek a career in such a business? One reason, says Katz, is that "living with the thought that you can get fired, or living with having to constantly present your soul in new-business presentations, is not a bad way to stay fresh, flexible, inventive. But," she adds, "it's also a business that pays big dividends and one that can be very rewarding early on. I don't think there's any business where you can make as much money in as short a time as in advertising."

## Time for that Personal "Review"

A personal review may not be easy. It's never easy to be totally honest with ourselves about ourselves. But look at it this way: "If I am totally honest with myself, about myself, I stand a far greater chance of locating work that's so absorbing I'll never know what time it is," as Charlotte Beers describes it. Plus, you'll have done the sweat work in gathering a working list of characteristics, traits, virtues, attributes, and talents that can be sorted and re-sorted to come up with those best suited for each future job application you make as you climb the ladder.

And with all this information in hand, you can establish a brand identity that makes it easier for buyers to recognize you as the product they need and want for their agencies or in-house ad departments. You want to make it easier for advertising people to recognize that you are the person for whom they do handstands and jump through hoops to get on staff.

## Know "The Product"

Therefore your job, just as it is in the ad business, is first to check out everything about the product—you—even to the perceptions others have about you. In this case it means get the mirror out—and don't just glance at what is reflected there.

It's a little hard to believe, but this is the step most often ignored by job seekers—especially first-timers. Yet there's no other way to be able to fill a customer's wants or needs, and thereby get him or her to buy the product, if you don't know what the product has to offer. It provides the ammunition—what you can offer them—that will convince employers they need and want you.

Self-reflection has another purpose. When you know as much about yourself as possible, you'll have a pretty good idea about where in the business you want to be, what you want from the business, and then you can set the goals and objectives to get there.

To begin the process get the lined notepad out and begin by listing every skill, every ability, every talent, your likes and dislikes, your interests, aptitudes, expertise, strengths, and weaknesses. (Your lists of dislikes and weaknesses aren't for anyone else's eyes, but it's a must in helping you decide how a particular job will fit you.) Skills, abilities, and talents are somewhat synonymous. Skills are notable abilities that come from training and practice. Abilities extend beyond skill and come from tendencies and talents. Talents are natural abilities—something you were born with.

Think about your hobbies, the things you like doing away from work. They may not be directly marketable, but if an agency you're interested in joining now or down the line specializes in sports, your hobby can be a positive highlight in your "sales features." The same could be true of travel interests for specialist travel agencies. But list *all* of your hobbies. You may never know until you get inside how these can be useful in specific circumstances. They could be attributes that will influence a boss to let you work on an account or even on the presentation for a new account.

Computer skills are about as necessary these days as a college degree. And Web competence is almost a necessity. Today it's a whole new world with new-tech advertising setting the running pace. Advertisers are aggressively increasing their spending in cyberspace, and the big new ad tech is in Web ads. If you have computer and Internet knowledge, skills, and training, develop the information for prominent use in your resume and presentation. There's more about the necessity for and use of these skills in Chapter 11: Reaching Out to New-Tech Advertising.

Don't try to evaluate the items or sort them into categories until the list is complete. Don't rush it. And don't panic if it takes days or weeks to accomplish. And don't think only of technical skills. If this were a job hunt in most other fields, such things as artistic or creative ability or an ability to see the humor in seemingly unhumorous situations probably wouldn't be worth much to employers. In advertising however, both are considered talents—and priceless.

## Where's Your Passion?

"In many careers," according to Tony Robbins, "passion is the first key to success. In the ad business it's the only key to success. Without it, you need to try something else."

But first, figure out if you have the passion for advertising. Or for a particular venue within the field. In the ad business, it's essential to be passionate about what you're doing. And without conveying your passion to a potential employer, you may be passed over as just another applicant. Unfortunately, passion is something that can't be taught.

## Don't Just Rest on Your College Degree

A college program designed to outfit you for a career in advertising is pretty much a necessity these days. But in today's constantly changing advertising field, an advertising or marketing degree isn't particularly impressive to the professionals. That's because almost without exception, those with such degrees have been taught by professors never in or long gone from and out of touch with the advertising business, or by academics who are unable to give the depth and kind of instruction and training that is needed for performing on the firing line. Unless your courses were taught by people who remain active in advertising, you probably aren't truly up to date about what's happening in the business today, what an advertising agency does, what individuals in an agency do, what the interrelationship between departments is, and how it all comes together for the client. Even those just out of the business may be out of touch because the advertising business today is moving so fast it's almost impossible to keep up—unless you're actively in it on a daily basis. Yes, you need a degree, but your degree is not what a pro first looks for when scanning your book. Sorry.

With that in mind, you may do just as well with a degree in English that has prepared you to write well and think critically. Or you may be well situated with a degree in computer science, which will prepare you for jobs in the high-tech sector of advertising. You should, of course, list your degree and the kinds of information it includes, but don't count on it to be a serious factor in getting hired. Don't count on using it to top your list of qualifications.

On the other hand, if you have on-the-job training, perhaps acquired while working as a summer intern, that can be vitally important. List it, point out what kind of training it was, what you learned from it, and keep it high on your list.

## Catalog Strengths and Weaknesses

These lists are for your eyes only. So be brutally honest, even when it means owning up to what in some areas of the business are considered weaknesses, such as impatience with particulars and technicalities. Or a desire to remain in the background, out of the spotlight, away from face-to-face encounters.

List the things you do well. List what you like to do and why you like doing them. Are you good at thinking up new or different ideas? Or are you analytical, logical, and systematic? Do you work well as part of a team? Or do you prefer to work alone? List your personality characteristics—both positive and negative—such as assertiveness and aggressiveness or a domineering nature, persistence or inflexibility, leadership or subordination.

A quality sought by every employer on the planet is *honesty*. But one of J. D. Crowe's comic strips in his "Non Sequitur" strip may give you pause about being ground-level honest about everything in your resume. The applicant sits before a personnel interviewer and says, "You certainly win points for honesty. Now, how often do these 'blind fits of homicidal rage' occur?" Well, you get the point!

There's also a point to be made for some "weaknesses" in this stay-on-your-toes-every-minute business. If, for example, you become bored easily, that can be a trait that's considered a plus in the ad business. If you want to use it, don't top your qualities list with it—and be sure it's worded delicately, and show how it works in pushing you to come up with ideas or alternatives or solutions.

## What Impresses the Pros

Valuable characteristics in ad people include:

- A passion for embracing the business
- Curiosity that reaches into what amounts to research to find out about a client's competition
- Familiarity with new developments, previous and present products or services
- Creativity and imagination

- Enthusiasm to a degree that stamina for working long hours is essential
- Motivation that includes initiative and a willingness to offer ideas, ability to originate and take action
- Team spirit, because almost always advertising recommendations to a client represent the combined contributions of a number of people who represent different areas of the agency

## SETTLE DIFFERENCES

The easiest way to get your list together is first, mentally, to go around to the other side of the desk. Take a notepad and pen with you. In this boss's seat—the seat where a potential employer sits while taking a look at you—it's easier to assess all that you need to know about yourself from that employer's viewpoint. And this process can't be stressed too much because it's only about what the organization needs and wants and is interested in. This is what you need to lay out on the table for him or her, not what you want. Of course, during the interview you may be asked what you want—so you must know that answer, too.

The boss's seat is also the place to sit to evaluate your difference(s) from others who are also competing for a particular position, so you can show how your difference(s) will benefit each employer.

When your list is complete, hang onto it. Save yourself the time and energy of having to do it again when and if you decide to move up, around, or out of the advertising business. Months or even years later, undoubtedly most of these strengths will be there just as they are today. The bulk of the analysis will already be done, and updating will be far easier than starting all over again.

## THE PURPOSE OF ALL THIS SELF-ANALYSIS

Self-analysis is the camera or CAT scan that gives you a picture of the kinds of jobs you'll enjoy most and the responsibilities for which you're best suited. It's also an MRI that reveals your deficiencies or weaknesses. With that knowledge, you can work to improve or replace them, or work around them.

All this preparation is necessary groundwork to help you determine the job zone within the advertising business in which you want to land. (To check potential choices, refer back to Chapter 4: Kinds of Jobs in Advertising.)

It also will help you decide whether an agency is right for you, whether you want to join a big agency or a smaller one, and it will help you determine when an agency is *not* for you. You might determine that you'd prefer to kick off a career working for an in-house advertising department or as a member of a core resource group offering specific services. (Chapter 3: Three Routes to Get You There, gives you applicable information about agencies, in-house ad departments, and core resource groups.)

## Do You Fit the Pattern?

There's no challenge to the belief that advertising is a different kind of business. It attracts highly unique and singularly different types of temperaments and natures. One pro goes so far as to say that the business attracts "a rich and varied cast of characters. It attracts some funny people." However, he also notes that "there is room for them all, and small fortunes for the lucky ones."

It's important to recognize that this business is made up of a complex variety of jobs, which require different skills—and very different personalities. The best agencies *do* include an immense range of people-types, skills, and talents. However, there is agreement among highly successful professionals that the people most likely to succeed, regardless of the area of occupation they choose, and who are able to really enjoy the business are those who have several things in common—enthusiasm, initiative, vitality, drive, motivation, and ambition. Just as is true for any career success story, right?

For those who dislike routine, advertising can be *the* place to be. Each client's needs are different, and each assignment is different from every other assignment. Variety and change are constants. For those who want consistency and constancy, the ad business may not be the best fit.

There's another must to ensure a good fit—team spirit. Clients' problems and solutions are considered and solved by groups within the agency who put their heads together and come up with recommendations and direction that are most likely to create success. Just about all of it is teamwork, so the ability to get along with people is essential.

## What Your MRI Shows

Here are four important questions you can ask yourself in order to determine whether you fit in this industry. They all evolve around one question: Can you adapt . . .

- To hectic schedules?
- To working with a group?
- To pressures to produce?
- To a lack of working privacy?

These are important questions because almost everyone can adapt. In these circumstances, however, people sometimes think that what they must have is only what they've gotten used to. Adapting is almost always a possibility *if* there's desire and *if* there's motivation.

Be totally honest in your self-assessment. If there are things to which you just can't adapt, steer clear of those areas. Choose to go after only the areas in advertising that fit your personal wants, needs, and requirements—not always an easy thing to do when just getting a job, any job, seems imperative at the moment.

## ESTABLISH A BRAND IDENTITY

In advertising, a brand is considered a company's or product's name, a graphic image associated with the company, what the company does. When it's put together, it's known in the business as a *unique selling proposition*, or USP.

That's exactly what you want to establish for yourself—a USP that allows you to stand out from your competition, that may even be unique enough to make you completely singular but that definitely ensures you will be remembered and stand apart from all the other aspirants.

When you've decided what your brand identity is, you can and should use it at every opportunity in your job search—in letters, presentations, leave-behinds, follow ups—to reinforce the message you want delivered.

## TESTIMONIALS ARE ENDORSEMENTS

Testimonials are a power force in advertising. You should start collecting them now. If you begin gathering your testimonials *now*, you'll have them in hand when you're ready to put your campaign together. Call on your college instructors who actually are card-carrying members in the advertising profession. Or, if you've done some OJT in any advertising situation, ask the company or department head or supervisor for whom you worked for a few words of approval on your behalf. These words, from professionals, will carry weight with professionals. Later, you'll use them in a number of ways as you put your presentation together and write the necessary letters.

Here's an idea! How about gathering your testimonial sentences and designing an ad that uses a few of the best of them—about you! Such an insertion in your presentation or as an attachment to your resume could do three things: condense them into an attractive, readable format, separate and make them stand out from the rest of the presentation or resume, and get the customer to actually read the affidavits about you.

What you're looking for are snippets of praise about you that will attract and pull in that indifferent customer.

Here are the basics for such an ad, and in the next section we give an actual example of a testimonial ad from FastSigns.

- Use a compelling—from the consumer's point of view— testimonial as a headline. If none of those you've gathered is sufficiently forceful, pick the one given by someone whose name, title, or affiliation is most respected and recognized for your headline, and display the person's name prominently.

- List other statements in the order of their importance. Just don't use so many that the reader is turned away.
- Include the name—and *affiliation*—of the person giving the statement, under each one.

## A Testimonial Ad

FastSigns has grown from a single test store in 1985 to a rapidly growing international franchise network of 390 stores that has been named the number-one business-to-business franchise in America. Much of its success can be attributed to letting their target audience know the pats on the back they've been given, which establishes image and credibility as well as support and satisfaction by franchisees.

The ad's headline—which occupies about one third of the magazine's page—is a testimonial from one of its own:

*When one franchiser stands out so far ahead of the rest, you get on that winning team.*
—Dwight Harts
FastSigns Franchisee
Denver, Colorado

The body copy consists of four more signed affidavits from prominent trade publications, such as *Entrepreneur* magazine. Even the small type below the company's logo, address, and 800 number tends to increase respect for the company's growth potential. It states:

*For international franchise opportunities in Argentina, Australia, Brazil, Columbia, Mexico and the United Kingdom, as well as master franchise opportunities in other countries, phone (800 and fax numbers).*

Choose your testimonials carefully, but don't be afraid to brag. After all, the bragging *about* you is done by people with respected names or affiliations, not *by* you.

## Humor Them

Humorous testimonials can be highly effective. If you have difficulty gathering verifiable commendations, you might dream them up as proof of your ability to use humor. Remember that everyone loves humor, and perhaps you can take an idea from the *Gone Fishin'* movie ads. They tickled a lot of funny bones, were absolutely and obviously fictitious, and undoubtedly convinced many people to see the movie. The headline reads,

### *"HOLY MACKEREL—YOU'LL LAUGH YOUR BASS OFF!"*
—The Sandshark Sentinel

Four "testimonials" follow:

### *"Thank cod for this movie!"*
—Saturday Evening Pike

### *"See it just for the halibut!"*
—The Walleye Weekly

### *"Bring your whole grouper to this movie!"*
—Barnacle and Seaweed Monthly

### *"You'll have a whale of a good time!"*
—The Clam Chronicle

Dream up your own statements of personal praise, tint them with a bit of humor, or perhaps quote some long-dead historical figures telling how important you were to the advertising for their cause, in achieving their goals, in picturing their concepts. Be sure, though, that the recipient knows this is a spoof; choose only names everyone knows are long gone from the planet.

Such inventiveness just may give your prospective boss an insight into a priceless ability or a sense of humor he or she might not otherwise realize you have.

## IF YOU'RE NOT SURE

What if you're not sure advertising is where you want to be? There's really only one way you're going to get an answer to this question. Try it on and see if it fits.

With the self-evaluation you've done, you undoubtedly are able to tell whether you have the attributes that are required to be successful. But a definite yes or a final no to the question isn't wise until after you've done a little wading. There's such a broad range of occupations within the advertising field that you undoubtedly can find an area for which you have a passion and in which you'll be completely happy, although it may take some snooping and switching before you're absolutely sure.

At one end, there are areas that require the most structured minds, such as accounting, traffic, research, and media buying. At the other end, creativeness and free-thinking are essential for such challenges as copywriting, art and graphics, and production. You may find, after dipping your toes in the water, that you belong in the advertising business, but you belong in a different area from the one(s) you're now considering. This is why exploration of each department, what each one does, how they do it, and what abilities and attitudes are required is not only important to becoming an active member of a team but in showing you where you best fit on that team. Before you're able to get that inside look, read or reread Chapter 4 about the kinds of jobs available in advertising, and use it as a checklist to at least explore all the areas that sound interesting and inviting.

## CHOOSE THE JOB ZONE AND SET SOME GOALS

You've heard this advice in one form or another until you're sick of hearing it. Yet common sense tells you you definitely must know what you want to do, where you want to go, and that you must set the goals, with objectives, that will get you there.

In 1992, Robert McGarvey said in an article in *Reader's Digest* that "we all have dreams and desires, but relatively few people have goals." That's scary! Without goals, without identifying what you want, how will you ever know where you want to go, or when you've arrived? What a waste of a life!

George Eld, back in the early nineteenth century, made a very wise observation—a secret for achievement:

The first two letters of the word goal spell GO.

It's time to GO, so let's start setting your goals. Remember that there are short-term, mid-term, and long-term goals, that they should be reevaluated on a regular basis, and that any of them can be adapted or changed at any time if a change in desire or direction happens. We're concerned with the short-termers here, but it's the long-termers that dictate short- and mid-term goals, because they are what get you to that ultimate, coveted, up-the-ladder destination.

## The Goal Standard Is Highly Objective

Whoa! Before we take off on this mission, let's get something out in the open. People talk about goals *or* objectives. But there's a whole lot more to it.

There are both goals *and* objectives, and they are not synonymous in the way so many people use them. They are equally important, but oh so different. A person first expresses his or her aims in terms of goals. Then he or she creates the *objectives* to achieve the goals.

A Charles Schwab commercial says, "Part of setting a goal is finding a way to reach it." To find the way to reach it you must set objectives. It is important to have well-expressed goals, but the goals will just sit there and accomplish nothing unless you spell out—in objectives—how to achieve the aspirations.

A *goal* is a statement of broad direction or interest, which is general and timeless, and is not concerned with a particular achievement within a specified time period. It is a long-range plan that can be lofty but not unrealistic. It's determined by needs. It must be attainable, though, as in this example.

My goal is to acquire a good-paying job in copywriting in the advertising business in an area where I enjoy the work and with a smaller agency where I can get an overview of the entire business.

*Objectives* pin down that broad, general, timeless aspiration and get it accomplished within a specific time period. *Objectives* are the explicit specifications for an end result. They must be practical, specific, and attainable, but set to require some "stretching and reaching." The heart of an objective is specificity. Each objective must be measurable.

Within six months of this date, I will acquire an entry-level copywriting job, paying at least $00,000, with a local agency that specializes in sports and sports equipment or that handles at least one account of this type, so that my interest, experience, and sports abilities can be used effectively.

A good way to remember what an objective must do is with the S-M-A-R-T acronym. It must be:

S — specific
M — measurable
A — achievable
R — reasonable
T — timed (accomplished within a designated time period)

## Get in Shape to Set Clients' Goals

An added benefit of this very personal exercise is that it will also work for you within the business of advertising. Recognition of the tremendous importance of objectives in management has led to the widespread practice of management by objectives among highly successful enterprises. These enterprises just may be clients of an agency you break into.

Or, who knows. The targeted company with an in-house advertising department or the agency you're aiming to join may practice management by objectives, and your knowledge of it can be a big plus for you. In this management concept, each manager has predetermined results, usually measurable, that are expected to be achieved within a given period for which the manager is fully responsible and is evaluated on the success of achieving the expected results.

You can be absolutely sure, however, that the advertising agency and every one of its clients have both goals and objectives (though they may call them something different) for every project they work on.

Just as is true for your own goals and objectives, those written for clients must be explicit, precise, and capable of being evaluated as to results or the potential for results within specified time periods. The writing of clients' goals and objectives, however, should be in far more interesting and attractive language. In other words, make it sound good for an agency client. For yourself—or for the ad agency you'll be working for—make it realistic!

You've done the hardest part of the break-in plan. Now let's check out the customer in Chapter 6.

# chapter 6

## Step 2—Know the Customer

It's time to go fishing!

But where? For what kind of fish? And are they biting? On what kind of bait?

Not even first-time fishermen would pick up a rod and reel and drive down the road hoping to find some water to drop the hook and line in. Nor would they try to catch saltwater fish in a freshwater lake. That's just common sense. So, let's use some of that same common sense to find where the kinds of fish you want to catch are and what kind of bait attracts them.

In advertising and marketing this step is called *niche marketing* or *target marketing*. It's the strategy used to dig out a narrow market segment that research indicates would be responsive to a particular product or service, determine that it wants or has need for the product or service, or has already purchased a competitor's brand.

Sometimes a *single niche* produces too few fish. *Entrepreneur* magazine learned it's possible to target too narrowly when they published *Entrepreneurial Woman* magazine. Rieva Lesonsky, editorial director, explained that "women business owners, we discovered, wanted their entrepreneurial information presented in the more general format of *Entrepreneur* [magazine], rather than in the specialized *Entrepreneurial Woman*."

Businesses and job-seekers can become too "niche minded," as *Entrepreneur* discovered. That's when, in advertising and marketing, *multiple niching* is necessary. To locate an adequate number of prospective consumers, you, too, may have to broaden your target base, develop multiple niches—specialty agencies, general agencies of a certain size, those in specific geographic areas, companies with in-house departments, agencies, and/or companies that have entry-level positions.

## KNOW THE REAL CUSTOMER

In 1992, Bill Whitehead drew a cartoon for *Advertising Age*. The graphic shows a couple at dinner. He reaches across the table, holds her hand and says, "Margaret, I want to know the *real* you . . . subject to a sampling error of plus or minus 3 percentage points, of course."

Forget the error factor here. What you want right now is to get to know the real customer, the one who will hire you because your skills, abilities and talents are *needed*. Actually, you must make them want those aptitudes, too. Rieva Lesonsky ended one of her "Speaking Out" columns with solid advice meant for entrepreneurs, but which you can modify to your position. She said, "You don't make money giving people what they need. You have to give them what they want." Change the sentence to read, You don't *get a job just* giving people what they need . . . and, we add, if you can make them *want* it so bad they believe they *need* it, you've got yourself a buyer.

So now you must answer the most important question in the entire process: What are you going to do for customers that's better or different than what your competitors are doing?

That's your biggest challenge, says Rob Fey, author of *The 200 Minute Marketing System* (Fey Marketing, Inc., 1997). He offers a step-by-step process for answering the question, including:

- Define your core competency. In other words, don't try to be everything to everyone, "be significant to a very specific audience."
- Choose a market focus. Zero in on your primary market.
- Identify a dominant need.

This last step undoubtedly is the most important point to determine before you can decide what you can do better or differently from your competitors. What dominant need does the agency you're targeting have? And what skills, abilities, talents, and expertise do you have that will help fill that dominant need?

## Another Synonym?

So many words and trades have become synonymous in people's minds—such as advertising and marketing. Here are a couple more—customer and consumer—used throughout this book with reference to product or service buyers as well as to buyers of your product.

"Customer" is better understood and used more often than "consumer" by most people, but in this situation, both terms apply. Retail icon Stanley Marcus simplifies the distinction. He says a consumer is a statistical abstraction; a customer is a human being. You need to think in both terms while studying your competition. Give them the facts, Ma'am, but never forget you're in contact with *human beings*.

With regard to your break-in to advertising, the customer is the person who purchases the product or service (the big boss). The consumer then, is the end user—the person who actually uses the product or service but wasn't necessarily the buyer (the creative director, the media buyer, the head of research or of traffic or any of the other departments). Mainly though, you'll find the two words used throughout this book as virtual synonyms in most references to potential employers.

## Know Your Customers as Intimately as Possible

Success is delivering to the customer exactly what he or she wants. But how do you know what *your* customer wants? In marketing language, determining this is called "research and data."

One thing you have to remember when you're dealing with people—they're all different. The same holds true for ad agencies, corporate ad departments, and individual support resource groups. It takes effort to dig out what those differences are, and to develop the appeal(s) that will cause the customer to buy. But the added benefit is that then you can line up your findings and zero in on only the places where *you* want to be, where *you* will fit in and be comfortable, and where *you* can learn what you need to know in order to move up, around, or perhaps even move out of advertising and into another field.

## Don't Take Anything for Granted

Bet you didn't know that mature adults who subscribe to *Modern Maturity* go for fast food more often than teenagers! When the magazine's research department turned up data showing that more than 226,947,000 times a month their "mature" readers head for a fast-food restaurant, and that this number is substantially larger than the number of teens who frequent fast food places, they turned it into a search-for-advertisers ad. The magazine used the tag line, "Serve your advertising up to hungry people in *Modern Maturity*."

The message here is, don't take anything for granted—whether it's that teenagers eat more hamburgers than older people or that the companies you'll be targeting are mostly like all the others in the business, and they all want the same type of employee.

Perhaps the best way to find out exactly what your customers think and want is to look around and *listen*. When VW started listening to customers again back in 1993 and 1994, they discovered why their sales and market share had plummeted. They had killed the Beetle, once America's most popular import. When they checked, they found that a used Beetle, in good condition, was selling for more than it did when it was new. So what did they do? They reintroduced the Beetle—but it took them until 1998 to get around to it.

It was not only research VW used. They checked out their would-be customers, and they *listened*. "Market research only measures conventional wisdom," says Oren Harari, a university business professor. And then he says the most profound words of all: "If your product or service [you] is truly innovative, people probably don't know they want it yet."

Do you have something to offer that is unique, innovative, or just plain hard to find among the pool of people available to agencies? If so, recognize they may not realize they want/need it yet, so you must use tactics similar to those used in the advertising business to drum a point home and develop demand.

## Narrow the List

Reduce the effort required to gather your niche market group before you begin by narrowing the areas where you'll conduct your search. Some of the zones can be eliminated merely by simple decisions made in advance.

- What geographical area do you want to be in? Along one of the coasts? In the heartland? The southwest desert area? Hill or mountain country? It doesn't matter?
- Do you like New York–size cities? Dallas or Atlanta size? Or a small town where most people know each other?
- Do you think you'd like working in a big corporation, a big agency? Or would you like the more friendly "intimacy" of a small agency where you get to know everyone—and must get along well with everyone—the bosses, co-workers, clients?

Your answers will dramatically tailor your list.

Later, when you've made these initial list-cutting decisions, there are other questions that will narrow the index even more. Here are a couple to keep in mind.

- Is it important to find a company where OJT (on-the-job training) is offered? And finally the biggest question of all:
- What is the lowest salary you will/can accept? What salary would you like to receive?

## ABOUT SALARY

*Advertising Age* compiled a list of salary ranges at the end of 1997 for a handful of entry-level positions. They found that employment placement agencies and college placement offices say "job-hopefuls with solid [undergraduate or postgraduate] internship experience stand a better chance at landing the job itself, if not higher pay. MBAs with that kind of experience can expect salaries in the $45,000–$65,000 range. Entry-level agency salaries for an assistant media planner/traffic coordinator was between $17,500 and $22,500. For an assistant account exec, $20,000 to $25,000. For an account exec/media desk coordinator, $27,500 to $32,500.

## A Roundup of the Range in Agency Salaries in 1997

(By agency size—between $3.6 and $45 in millions of gross income)

| | | | |
|---|---|---|---|
| Copywriter: | From | $ 42,000 | to $ 60,000 |
| Art Director: | From | $ 46,500 | to $ 57,100 |
| Creative Director: | From | $ 75,700 | to $156,200 |
| Account Executive: | From | $ 36,200 | to $ 37,100 |
| Media Director: | From | $ 42,100 | to $ 92,400 |
| CFO: | From | $ 56,700 | to $135,600 |
| COO: | From | $ 95,600 | to $241,700 |
| CEO: | From | $108,700 | to $250,000 |

Source: AM&G Survey for *Advertising Age*

## WHERE TO FIND "FISH BITING" LISTS

Okay. It's time to stop calling prospective employers "fish."

This is where we must narrow down the possibilities because it's much better to concentrate the search, just as for an advertising campaign. In your case, narrow it to just ten, perhaps twenty prospects, who are likely to want or need your abilities and who fit your needs and wants.

Begin with the *Standard Directory of Advertising Agencies* (also known as the *Agency Red Book*). It lists thousands of advertising agencies. It also has breakout sections listing House Agencies, Media Buying Services, and Sales Promotions Firms. But perhaps its most valuable section for your purposes is the Agency Responsibilities Index, which sorts the names of people working in the field into the division categories where they work. The list includes account coordinators, account directors, account executives, account supervisors, art directors, creative, media directors, media planners, new business contacts, print production, sales promotion, and traffic.

This is valuable because when you're ready to launch your campaign you will have the *actual names* of the people who head up divisions in which you want to work, whom you can personally address. However, when you're ready to contact the people, be sure to call the agencies to validate that the persons listed in the directory still work there. People change jobs in every type of business, but no business is more fluid than advertising. And no replacement person enjoys getting mail addressed to a predecessor, which automatically puts a negative stamp on anything you send.

Your local library may have a copy of this directory. If not, try calling a local advertising agency and ask if you may come in and consult their copy. This can be a great way to get an inside glance at an agency you think may show up on your target list. It may also be an opportunity to get a look at a few of the people who work there.

Another excellent resource that may supply additional information is *Adweek's Directory of Advertising*. It's a series of six regionalized books on agencies, clients, media companies, and service companies. The regions the books cover are New England, East, West, Midwest, Southeast, and Southwest.

All this information, when eventually sorted and narrowed down to your best estimate of your target market, is comparable to a database developed by an agency for its clients.

## Tips for Identifying Your Target Group(s)

A list is just a list. It's only names and addresses. How do you dig out the agencies or the companies with in-house departments that are best for *you?* And the information about them that brings them to life?

- First, gather from all available sources (your local library may have directories or resources beyond *The Red Book* and *Adweek's Directory of Advertising*) from which to assemble the names of potential employers in the fields of advertising that interest you.
- Check out the competition. Tap your fellow advertising or marketing friends or graduates for information and where they're conducting their searches. There may be a hot market you aren't aware of. Or this may tip you to an area where there may be too many soliciting a group, so it would be best to look to other fields.
- Ask a college or university instructor for access to brochures, letters, or any job applications he or she has collected. They may reveal the people and places that you may want to add to your database—or avoid!
- Talk with people who hire advertising agencies and get as much information as possible about their agency's services, the people who represent them, and what impresses them about the agency and its people. This kind of information— both positive and negative but probably without naming names—possibly can later be worked into your presentation to demonstrate the depth of your interest and preparation and perhaps with suggestions for a unique or different way of handling an assignment. (It also could end up in a letter of introduction on your behalf to their agency. Don't be reluctant to ask for advice and help. Most people truly enjoy offering helpful information and lending a hand to someone who is sincere, pleasant, and *appreciative*.)
- Read the trades, such as *Advertising Age* and *Adweek*. Keep abreast of what's happening in the industry as well as noting names to contact. These are vital, constant sources for locating new opportunities and gathering information about agencies, companies, people, products, and services. The trade press, the *New York Times'* daily Media Business and Advertising sections, and occasionally your local newspaper's business pages are where you'll learn when a new agency comes on the scene or an agency opens a

branch office in a geographical area in which you're interested. They also are where the acquisition of new accounts is reported—which can be an indication that these agencies are hiring.

## Finding the Good Agencies

Advertising notable Ronald Scharbo, quoted from the *Advertising Career Directory* (Gale Research, 1993), has excellent advice about the characteristics to look for in your search for an agency.

- A healthy mix of good people and the right attitude. Bad account people can cancel out good creative people, and vice versa.
- Management's commitment to always doing better work.
- The courage to take risks . . . and the ability to go easy if one fails.
- Involvement of the creative people in the research mechanism.
- AEs who are teammates, not adversaries.
- Client involvement—before, during, and after the fact. No matter what ad execution an agency hopes to do, it can't be done unless the client supports the effort. The agency has to sell them.
- Appreciation of the people who make things happen. Management should know who the champions are, not just in creative, but throughout the entire agency. Find out how they acknowledge good work—in person, in memos, in public, etc.

## DETERMINE THE CUSTOMER'S NEEDS

There are two reasons consumers buy: they *need* the product and/or they *want* the product.

In the broad public marketplace, what people *want* can be very strong buying motivators. People buy luxuries or things they like or desire. In this case, however, want is rarely a serious motive for an advertising organization to "buy" an individual's abilities and talents. Every hire must be justified in terms of whether that person's services will pay off. An agency or an in-house advertising department must *need* you, particularly the skills and abilities you have that they don't have, or that they're short on because they've just acquired a new account.

If their agency has followed the new downsizing trend, if they are operating what advertising authority Ray Champney calls a virtual agency, and mainly use support resources rather than maintaining in-house departments, they may have no need for copywriters, production people, artists, or media buyers. Any effort to get on with these agencies is a waste of time because almost all of their work is done by outsiders who are called on to produce on a per-project basis.

## Even the Pros Sometimes Don't Know

There's belief that as many as two thirds of companies fail to recognize their customers' needs because they rely on perceptions rather than facts.

Good research often is born after the fact—to learn what went wrong. In your case that may be too late. If you don't know what your customer wants, and you make the wrong pitch, it's almost a sure bet you won't get the chance to do the after-the-fact research that agencies and companies do and then come back with a new campaign. For the companies, after-the-turn-down research usually doesn't work too well either, but they usually make the effort. Many months and many, many advertising and marketing dollars later, they may manage a turnaround. You won't get the same chance.

## Get a Look Inside

Of course you can go the cold turkey route. You may have to, using only the information you can pick up from outside sources. But there's nothing as valuable as first getting inside for a look around.

Earlier we suggested contacting a local agency to locate a copy of *The Agency Red Book* to check for some of your research. That, indeed, is a reason to go inside an agency. The more you know about a company, the more effective and impressive your presentation can be. Some of the information to look for includes:

- Does the agency depend heavily on support resources? Or does the group have in-house functions. Which ones?
- What interrelationships are there between these departments? How do they mesh? What are the contributions the departments make toward the big picture?
- Is it a place where you can become a specialist in one area and a generalist in all areas?

It undoubtedly will take a little ingenuity to get this kind of information. You certainly must not give the appearance of prying or snooping. But showing a sincere interest in the company through any questions you may ask of those you come in contact with, and an explanation to those you talk to, that the business of advertising and working in it is a passion for you may even elicit enthusiasm on their part to help you.

## Getting Inside Pays Off

Cheryl Hall, an editor for the *Dallas Morning News*, tells about an advertising executive whose modus operandi demonstrates the payoffs from doing inside investigations. It might work for you if you dare to imitate.

Deb Gugel is the founder and president of Dallas-based Gugel Advertising. When she takes on a retail store as a client, she goes to the store, finds a cash register, and stands there to see how long it takes to get waited on. At a restaurant, "she checks out its ladies' room at high noon. Then she grabs a Diet Coke, sits amid the midday hubbub and observes," says Ms. Hall. All this is done as part of finding the best medium for her client's messages. And her clients say with appreciation that she spends every dollar of their advertising money as if it were coming out of her own pocket.

That's the tip for you. Check out every one of your prospective customers/clients as thoroughly as possible. And if possible, check out each client's clients. This will put you in the position that, when you prepare your presentation and have your interview, you can include information about *them* (and possibly their clients) that your competition hasn't a clue about. Count on it to impress the agency people. Further, it will give you a better perspective about working for them.

The bottom line is—Use every method you can dream up to narrow your job hunt to only a few organizations, then really go after them in an informed, personal way.

# chapter 7

## Step 3—Know the Competition

The ad business is all about competition. Learn to live with it and it will serve you well in the challenge to reach your goal. Equally important, it will remain as a large plus after your break-in, as well as in your climb up the ladder.

You may feel you have enough to do before you can go after those essential interviews without taking on this task of learning about people who are or will be competing against you. Or that acquiring the information about your competition is impossible because you have no idea where to look.

This step is essential, however, because your success depends on identifying—and standing out from—your competitors. Help in where to look, and find, the information you seek comes in this chapter.

### WHY BOTHER?

As we said, the ad business is all about competition. That also goes for breaking into the ad business, or any other job hunt, for that matter. It's essential to know and understand your direct competition and to use it exactly as successful ad pros do, to improve the product—you, to better "position the product" on the success ladder, and then, like every good salesperson, to tell your prospects the benefits and advantages they receive from buying this product rather than that of your competitor.

Back in January of 1995, Kmart made headlines in *Advertising Age* when it began its search for a new ad agency. "Kmart wants to be in control versus having to react to what our competition is doing," said the corporation's executive VP, marketing/product development, Kenneth Watson. Words to remember! Words that justify the time and effort spent to do this aspect of the research.

More research? Research has such a lousy reputation. Too many people say it's so dull and structured that only nerds and geeks can find fun in it. Actually, it can be one of the most exciting areas in advertising. It means digging out little-known, perhaps spicy information about the competition, about new, perhaps yet unknown new actions, tactics, and strategies. It can give you the upper hand.

Back to Kmart and its actions with regard to its competition. Kmart had had seven consecutive quarters of downward earnings, according to *Advertising Age*. And their foremost competitors—Wal-Mart Stores and Dayton Hudson Corp.'s Target Stores—had definitely proved they knew what they were doing. Wal-Mart was firmly positioned as the leading value-priced merchandiser, and Target had established a well-received, financially successful, trendy identity.

Watson told *Advertising Age*, "I am a firm believer that an advertising agency is not just someone who produces nice ads, but who can assist and help a corporation to strategically position itself."

## STRATEGICALLY POSITION YOURSELF

Analyzing the competition—whether done by a product or service company, by an advertising agency, or by an individual—is done primarily to create a winning strategy. It's done to put you more in control versus having to react to what your competition is doing, and so you will be able to *strategically position yourself*.

In business there are other reasons for being intimately familiar with the competition: if you don't know what your competitors are offering and what they're doing, you'll know less than your customers know. You won't know whether you're over- or under-pricing. And, if you're not aware when your customers respond to a competitor's buying appeal(s), how can you react quickly, adjust your advertising appeals, and get those customers' attention back?

All this is applicable to your job search. You want to know what are your competitors' attributes? In education, abilities, skills, temperament, teamwork? What you must go up against? All of it is information that's valuable in developing your competitor profile—and useful in understanding how the ad business recognizes and understands ways to overcome competitive obstacles.

According to Kim T. Gordon, president of National Marketing Federation and writing in *Business Start-Ups* magazine, analyzing the competition will reveal your competitors' key selling points and the expectations they've raised among your target audience. You'll learn their strengths and weaknesses and discover which niches are being served and which are not. Without this information it's virtually impossible to create a winning strategy.

## Have You Heard? Competition is Dead!

James Moore even wrote a book, *The Death of Competition* (HarperCollins Publishers, 1997), and he tells business leaders around the country, "Competition is dead!" But when *Entrepreneur* magazine interviewed him he admitted that "obviously, competition is not going away. In fact, it is intensifying. But the way in which we have been trained to think about competition—which is to see it as head-to-head [confrontation]—is dead."

His contention is worth tucking in the back of your mind for later when you've accomplished your break-in. And you can use it here as a reminder that *smearing* the competition *is* dead, particularly when the competition is a person rather than a product. More about that later, though.

Instead of a head-to-head smear campaign, focus on your competitive edge. Or take *Advertising Age*'s Bob Garfield's advice to former anchor Charlie Gibson on *Good Morning America* and recognize you have two choices: "You can come up with some kind of a benefit—often phony—that your competition doesn't have. Or you can entertain!"

## WHAT EMPLOYERS LOOK FOR

Training in specific areas of advertising is the first thing a potential employer looks for. If you're looking to break into copywriting, graphics or production, account management, accounting, or research, you must indicate that you have appropriate training or at least a proclivity for the field.

However, if you don't have a degree in advertising or special training, it's still possible to get hired. The two things you must show in addition to certain characteristics listed below, is a passion for the work and a willingness to log on as a trainee.

These are the most important characteristics, beyond training, that employers in the ad business look for:

- Enthusiasm
- Initiative
- Vitality
- Drive
- Motivation
- Ambition
- Team spirit and the ability to get along with and work with others

There's one more that's a real pleaser. A humor quotient.

As you check out the competition, try to assess which of these characteristics they *don't* have. Sort them out, and play up those you have that aren't predominant in others. Just be sure that your highlighted characteristics are those *needed* and *wanted* by the agency you're pitching.

## WHAT IF I CAN'T PINPOINT OTHERS' CHARACTERISTICS?

Okay. It may be nearly impossible to find out if each person you consider to be a competitor has these rather elusive attributes. But it's almost a guarantee that even if they have them, most won't think to list them. Or the ones they do detail are the ones *they're interested in*, not the ones that are of interest to the client. Therefore, it's fairly safe to proceed as if they *don't* have them or are short on them.

Start by listing your attributes and your differences from those of your competitors—and then dig out the ways *these differences benefit the employer.* This information, when completed, should be set aside until you're ready to put your presentation package together, when you'll show would-be employers the singular benefits you offer and how these benefits fit each so-called customer's needs and wants.

## WHERE TO LOOK

By comparison, it's relatively easy to check out the competition when it's a company or service that sells to the public. Checking out the people who may have an eye on the same jobs you're targeting is more difficult.

One of the best ways to get inside your competitors' heads—or at least to find out what they're up to—is to talk to the people at their university or college, to the people they work with, or to the people who work with the group they're pitching. This can work for you in another way, too. In smaller companies and advertising agencies, people who work there have a good idea when there's a search on for a new employee, when there's an opening, or even about in-house areas that need bracing up. They may be open to talking with someone—like you—who can show them the benefits that are wanted and needed. And they may even be willing to help you contact the proper person to listen to your presentation.

If the people you're researching are working, talk to their co-workers and, if possible, to their bosses. Even when they're not working in the advertising business, co-workers and bosses often can give you an insight into a person's abilities, dedication, and characteristics, which will give you a feeling for how strong your competition is. If they're still in or only recently out of a college, university, or a training institute, talk to their instructors.

What you want to know is their attributes—in education, abilities, skills, temperament, and teamwork.

## Visit the Target

In your customer search in Chapter 6, you got a pretty good line on who your targets are. Now go visit them. Receptionists and company telephone operators probably know more than anyone else about what's going on in a company. Drop by and have a chat.

Ask the person for advice. Then maybe for a little help. Most people enjoy helping others, and when the person asking for assistance is someone they react positively to, they're delighted to give a hand. Depending upon the size of the operation and the amount of communication between people within the company, the receptionist/phone operator may be able to put you in direct touch with an executive who is in a position to advise you and perhaps recommend you to the boss.

## BUSINESS ADVICE THAT CAN WORK FOR YOU

Guerrilla Marketing guru, Jay Conrad Levinson, uses *Entrepreneur* magazine to shout these words of wisdom to businesspeople: "Many of today's products and services are so similar to each other that the only difference is in their marketing."

If you could sit in a job interviewer's chair these days, you'd recognize how totally similar today's ad business job applicants are to each other. If that's a problem for you, the smart thing to do is hark to Levinson's words and dig until you find a marketing difference that will work for you. Competitive advantage is the trick that makes the difference, says Levinson. Convert and adapt his advice to your use: "If your widget doubles a company's profits, grows hair on bald heads, or attracts lifelong partners, you don't have to use gimmicks . . . Just the truth will do very nicely, thank you."

Then he goes on to say, "The idea is to identify your marketable competitive advantages, then concentrate heavily on those. If you don't have any marketable competitive advantages, know that a savvy guerrilla discovers them or creates them."

Equally applicable and *important* is another idea that Levinson puts forth—that of whether it requires a great deal of resources to achieve a competitive advantage. Not necessarily. "It takes brainpower, time, energy, and imagination, but it is not a matter of money," he says. Sometimes creativity can make up for where budgets fall short.

Go back and reread the Levinson advice as many times as it takes to get into the mode to proceed positively. As many times as it takes to recognize you have the brainpower and imagination it takes to convert your research into useful marketing, but you must dedicate the time and energy to do it.

Check the list of benefits that you can offer. Check off the benefits that are being offered by your competitors. Then check those they do not have, those that are most important to your prospect. These are your competitive advantages.

Use them and, as Levinson tells his audience, you too will have "a ticket to ride all the way to the bank." In your case, to the company chair that fits you best.

## ESTABLISH A TERRAIN OF YOUR OWN

Earlier, in Chapter 5, you began the job of establishing your brand identity, your USP—unique selling proposition. Now it's time to use it. This is an essential in advertising. And it's as big a plus as you could hope for in positioning yourself. It's the best way to outswim the competition, to stand out—way out—from rivals.

Each competitor in business may offer different benefits, though it's unlikely the majority of ad job applicants are this savvy. The successful businesses focus on single elements that attract the consumers *they* want and need. That way, each successful competitor is able to define a segment of its market and emerge with a distinct advantage over other contenders. Apply this strategy for your personal success.

One place to establish your own terrain may be with your knowledge about Net-literate advertising and/or your expertise in online work. The need now for Net savvy in most businesses, and certainly in the advertising business, is almost as necessary as a college degree. Forrester Research predicts Internet commerce will grow at a "breakneck pace"—from $8 billion in 1997 to $327 billion in 2002. The Web seems well on its way to becoming a mainstream medium, even though there seems to be a tendency among some advertising agencies to call on online specialty agencies rather than trying to handle it in-house.

With all the technologies just now coming across the horizon, there's need for totally new specialists. They're known as cyber-brains whose cyber-savvy trades off for much higher salaries. If you have this kind of expertise, flaunt it. It may be the competitive advantage that not only gets you an interview but gets you the job.

## Use Your Competitive Advantage to Position Yourself

As *The Marketing Glossary* (AMACOM Books, 1992) by Mark N. Clemente says in explaining positioning, "Developing a position-ing strategy is done after identifying the product's *competitive advantage* and determining the ways to best communicate it to the market." Positioning is thinking in reverse. Instead of determining how you think, how you feel, what you want and need, you start with how prospects think, feel, what they want and need.

Now is the time to determine what position you want to *own*. Yes, *own*! What you're on the road to accomplishing is establishing a position in the minds of those you'll be contacting for work. It's not to do the impossible—to preempt a position someone else already owns, but to find one that can be all yours.

Advertising authorities Al Ries and Jack Trout point out that Ford failed to position the Edsel successfully because there simply was no room in the mind of the auto buyer for another heavily chromed, medium-priced car. "On the other hand," they say, "when Richardson Merrill was trying to position an entry in the cold-remedy field against Contac and Dristan, it wisely avoided a direct confrontation. Leaving these two to fight it out in the daylight hours, Richardson Merrill chose to preempt the 'nighttime cold remedy' position for Nyquil."

## Head-to-Head Confrontation? No, No, No!

If someone out there already holds the edge on getting the position you desire, accept it and, as Ries and Trout recommend, "It's better to go around an obstacle rather than over it. Back up. Try to select a position that no one else has a firm grip on."

What you should *not* do is what is so prevalent in advertising today—put down the competition. If your competition is taking pokes at your strong points—probably because they can't boast the same advantages—resist getting down in the dirt with them.

Instead, turn their so-called advantages to your advantage, as some of the most successful advertisers have done.

Avis is number two in car rentals. Why? Because they try harder. Who can ever forget those ads, which actually are the presentation of their marketing strategy. Learn from their success. If you can't boast the greatest, the best, the most . . . pick something you're sure your prospects want and need or will react to strongly in a positive way. Trying harder did it for Avis.

## LOOK BEFORE YOU LEAP

Where do you look for information about your competition?

Networking groups may be your best bet. In Chapter 12, *Getting Ahead in the Industry*, the secrets of networking are set forth along with some how-tos. Advertising groups and associations are great places to find out who your competition is, what they're doing, and how they are perceived.

When you talk to these sources of information and contacts, be honest about what you want to know and why. It can't be said too often, people enjoy helping others when they respect and believe in the person asking for their help.

Then, once you get a lead, act on it *immediately*. Too many people ask for information or help, then sit back and do nothing. Don't bother to work the network if you're not willing to work the information.

# chapter 8

## Step 4—Develop a Plan

In Texas there are all kinds of expressions that tell you it's best to plan ahead: build the fence before you buy the horses; drill the well before you build the windmill; Noah built his ark before it started raining. And Hugh Roy Cullen said, "If you plan anything before you do it, you will usually come out all right. When you jump into anything without thinking about it ahead of time, you've got to trust to luck."

Sooner or later, once you're in the ad business, you'll need to understand plans and planning. A plan is the foundation of every campaign, whether it's to gain a client or work on behalf of a client. Without a plan, an ad campaign goes nowhere.

So, what better way to master planning and how it works than to develop a plan of your own that follows the canons of advertising—a plan to get you where you want to go in the advertising game. It certainly can be a plus with potential employers because they'll recognize the depth and focus you've used when they see the presentation that results from your plan.

There's groundwork to be done, however, before the plan can take shape. Positioning comes before all else.

## POSITIONING: WHAT YOU DO TO PROSPECTS' MINDS

Marketing executives were introduced to positioning by Jack Trout, president of Trout & Partners, a marketing consulting firm. In their book *Positioning: The Battle for Your Mind* (McGraw-Hill, 1969), Trout and coauthor Al Ries explained positioning as "what you do to the mind," not what you do to the product. It's an advertising strategy that is challenging to initiate, but it is necessary and productive because it's what influences how consumers perceive a product in relation to others in the same product category.

Here, positioning is necessary to influence how potential buyers perceive you and to set you apart from your competition.

Over the years the importance of positioning has grown—and changed somewhat. It has also changed the way the advertising game is being played today, says Trout. "Anyone can use positioning strategy to get ahead in the game of life. If you don't understand and use the principles, your competitors undoubtedly will."

Not only is it what advertising does to establish the product in prospective consumers' minds, it also "works to make the product fill all the needs of the consumer in a particular category or area," says Trout.

As we pointed out in the last chapter, the Avis slogan "We're Number 2" resulted in positioning Avis positively and permanently in the public's mind. At the same time that it established Avis's claims of better service and cleaner cars that are in better mechanical condition, it also took a huge bite out of Hertz's car rental earnings.

## Position Yourself

Jack Trout also was the one who suggested positioning strategies could and should be used to position individuals and their careers. Positioning not only can work for you, but it also serves the added purpose of familiarizing you with a proven method you must understand and use when you get your own chair inside an agency's or corporate ad department's doors.

All the product homework you've done: the lists of your talents, achievements, skills, abilities, strengths—even perhaps a weakness or two—are now ready to be sorted and used to position you in relation to what each consumer wants and needs and to set you apart from others who are competing for the same post.

It's time now to identify your *competitive advantage* and decide on the best way to get that information across to your target market—to that fine-tuned index you've developed, of people and places where you'd like to work.

As Jack Trout points out, too often advertisers try to make a product or a service be all things to all people. That was the accepted method in the days of mass marketing which, incidentally, has been bedridden for a number of years and is receiving assisted suicide advice from a public that very much prefers focused, targeted, one-to-one opportunities offered by new-tech advertising.

Sort through your list of attributes and isolate the skills, talents, and abilities that are most wanted or needed by that small group that is your niche market. Be objective. This has nothing to do with what *you* want or need. It must only consider what *they* need and want.

"The most difficult part of positioning [in advertising] is selecting that one specific concept to hang your hat on," says Trout. Yet that's the only way to go in advertising, and the recommended way to go in your break-in search. It may not be an easy job, but it will pay off big-time.

## CONCEPTING AND PLANNING COME NEXT

Former French President Georges Pompidou was known for saying, "Conception is much more fun than delivery." Indeed it is. The plan and delivery come later, but now it's time for you to start having fun—concepting!

Concepting is merely advertising jargon for finding that "brief basic idea for a campaign, product, show, or other work," according to *Webster's New World Dictionary of Media and Communications*. Concepting, like brainstorming, is best accomplished as a group effort. But, like brainstorming, it also can be done effectively by an individual.

### Make It a "Which Hunt"

Concepting in this case is deciding which information about the product, the customer, and the competition is important to your plan. It means sifting and sorting through your findings gathered in Chapters 5, 6, and 7 and deciding what to keep and what to leave behind. And it means using what you keep to come up with the best plan for this specific campaign to this niche market.

Don't throw anything away, however. Those findings, even the unused ones, may be exactly the information you'll want in future months or years, when you have another plan to put together to impress another customer, to capture another career maneuver.

## THE PLAN—THE BOARD'S PRAYER

There was a cartoon for the *Dallas Business Journal* by Jim Sizemore that recognizes the importance of a plan, but it also shows what often happens in planning sessions. The caption of the cartoon says, "Every company has one!" And it shows three people in session at the plans meeting. Instead of name cards there's an I.D. placard in front of each person: (1) short-range planning, (2) long-range planning, (3) harebrained schemes.

It's pretty obvious. Good planning sessions require only two agents on the committee. Actually, three: mid-range planning should be there, too. In your case, however, this session isn't meant to set up short- or long-range plans. Your objective is to develop a travel plan—the road map to get you there—and to uncover the opportunities, and problems, along the route.

So, what is a plan—at least in terms of the ad business? "The advertising plan is *not* a marketing plan," says Northwestern University professor Don E. Schultz in his book *Strategic Advertising Campaigns* (National Textbook Company, 1990). It is "an action document. [It] lists on paper all the steps that are to be taken." Agency advertising plans are detailed and formal. There's no need for your plan to include past records of programs that have been conducted. Nor is it necessary to specify who will be implementing and coordinating the various parts of the plan, since you're the one doing it all.

You will do well, however, to include a brief history or sketch of the agency you plan to target, it's history, and any pertinent issues that face the future of the agency and are relevant to its success.

In an advertising plan, there's a product evaluation, consumers' evaluation, and a competitive evaluation. You can adapt these to your use by including an evaluation of you—the product. The consumers' evaluation would be any and all testimonials you've managed to collect. And the competitive evaluation portion can be your comparison of your talents, abilities, skills, and so forth with those of others who are likely to be interested in the same agency job as you. This does not mean using personal comparisons; rather, note the likely deficiencies among your competitors.

## BRAINSTORMING IS THE EXERCISE OF THE PLANS TEAM

Plans preparation for a company or an advertising program is a group effort. As a member of a plans team in an agency, you may be asked to collect data, evaluate data, and participate in the actual planning process itself. You also undoubtedly will be asked to participate in brainstorming sessions. A Boeing commercial says, "Maybe one person can't do it alone—but together people can do anything."

In the advertising, business brainstorming is a way of life, though each agency may call it something else. It's not as unappealing as it sounds. It's merely asking for help. "Einstein, Edison, Jonas Salk, inventor of the polio vaccine, were among the thinkers who relied on group brainstorming," says Michael Michalko in his book, *Cracking Creativity* (Ten Speed Press, 1998).

### Call a Review Meeting

If you have mentors, you may want to invite them to participate in your planning brainstorm. But when these people aren't totally dedicated to your "cause" and aren't highly experienced in the way to contribute to such a meeting, it usually isn't very productive to include them.

It's generally true that the more participants the more ideas. But you may wish just to sit down alone with pen and paper and "noodle" some ideas on your own.

## New Exec Titles—and a New Name for Brainstorming

Every corporation has a CEO, a CFO, and perhaps a COO. But would you believe some, such as General Electric and the Young & Rubicam advertising agency, now have a CKO? That's a Chief Knowlege Officer! At Coca-Cola this new corporate position is called Chief Learning Officer (CLO?). It's a new job still in a developmental phase, but it is given executive status. Undoubtedly it involves much more than merely conducting brainstorming sessions. But you can be sure, when a CKO does call such a meeting it has a much more alluring name.

For some reason the term "brainstorming" is considered old-fashioned—so a new term has come about (probably birthed by a CKO): Articles of Speculation. It's the word "brainstorming," not the process, that is looked down upon. We'll settle for "brainstorming" though. It precedes every successful strategic plan—advertising or otherwise. Disney World uses it, and who can argue with a methodology that has produced Disney World's success?

But more important to you is the fact that agencies, such as Emmerling Post, use it. John Emmerling says it's their secret weapon. It's "a unique tool to jump-start the creative process; a way to use a single 4-hour session with a client to gain penetrating, powerful information about the product, the market, and the customers."

## Brainstorming Is . . .

". . . an example of a typical creative problem-solving technique," says Robert Fritz in his book *The Path of Least Resistance* (Fawcett Books, 1989). "Brainstorming is a process in which you attempt to blitzkrieg through your preconceived 'mind-set' by fanciful free association. The idea is to generate alternative solutions by overcoming your usual manner of thinking. You are encouraged to suspend your critical judgment so that you can be more inventive." Never turn it into a "blamestorming" session. Cut the negatives.

When a brainstorming session is a group meeting, there are just four rules, as follows:

1. Criticism or evaluation are ruled out. These tend to seriously cool enthusiasm or lead a person to defend rather than generate ideas.
2. Free-wheeling is welcomed. The wilder the idea, the better. It's easier to tone down an idea than to think one up.
3. Quantity, not quality, is wanted. The greater the number of ideas, the more likelihood of winners.
4. Piggyback or build on others' ideas. A really crazy idea may be the germ of a brilliant solution.

When you brainstorm by yourself, the same rules apply, except there's no opportunity to piggyback on others' ideas. Write down *everything* that occurs to you, then put the list aside for a couple of days. When you pick it up again you may be able to piggyback on one of your own ideas and find solutions for problems in your tentative plan.

## Mechanics for a Group Session Are Easy

1. Form your group. Any number from two to twelve is best.
2. Appoint a chairperson. Someone who can reduce the problem to *one* basic. Start it off with a question. "How" and "what if" questions are recommended. The chairperson literally rings a bell on negative thoughts, self-killer phrases, or tangential run-aways.
3. Appoint a secretary. Someone (nonparticipating) who can take down *every* idea, even repeated thoughts—not necessarily word-for-word but the concept of the idea. No editing here, either.
4. Set a time limit. For beginners it should be 20 minutes. The deadline is important because if there's a lull, it's natural to assume productivity is over and call it quits. Periods of silence usually are followed by great bursts of ideas, but if "dead air" produces restlessness, the chairperson should be prepared to toss in an idea or a question to trigger the group. A 20-minute session should produce from 50 to 150 ideas.

## Hold a "Hash Session"

After the storm has passed is when logical minds take over. This is the time when common sense, experience, and sound judgment come into play. Now is the time for judgments, such as whether an idea is practical or not, which one(s) have been tried before, what is too expensive, and so on.

The evaluation of ideas is as important as getting the ideas.

## There's Help Available

*Advertising Age*, in an insert it called "The New Wave: Technology and Change in Marketing," says there are all kinds of software that will facilitate creative brainstorming.

There are tools for both individuals and for groups for brainstorming and creative thinking. Particularly intriguing are small commercial expert systems in the under-$1,000 range that prompt users to think through ideas and ask questions about the ideas. They will reword what you have just said and use what you say to the computer to prompt you further to think about the ideas and to give you new ideas.

With your brainstorming done, it's time to *plan!*

## TO CORN A PHRASE . . .

"Don't start a vast project with half-vast ideas!" Whoever offered that advice must either have been one of those CKOs or just a regular advertising person trying to develop a campaign plan.

Here's a bit of guidance that successful planners pass along. Before you begin, find some ponder time—not only to sort out the half-vast notions, but to be sure about your direction. Now that you've conducted your "which hunt," sit back and ask yourself the big "why?" Why are you about to write this plan?

There's more than one reason in this case. Beyond the ultimate objective of finding the best way(s) to get you where you want to go, a plan offers an opportunity to learn and put into practice the essentials of planning that are indispensable when you become a team member in any advertising organization. It also is an investment of time and effort for the future. Your plan will be something to look back on so that you are able to assess the degree to which it has worked and to change those things that have changed or that didn't work. Do not—repeat, *do not*—set any plan, either for you or for an advertising client, in cement. Actually, it will require ongoing monitoring, even to the extent of each time you make a presentation as to the plan's effectiveness and any changes to make it more effective.

## COPYCAT—IT'S OKAY TO DO

A bit more advice: Copycatting—following someone else's plan design—is a good idea, *if* (big word here), *if* it can be tailored to *your* requirements. Actually, finding a plan that will work for you and then translating it into a purely personal one is the best kind of copycatting. This is a way to be sure your plan contains everything you need in order to translate it into *action*. And it's okay to copycat. The biggest ad agencies, product manufacturers, and TV entertainment programs do it.

Let's copycat from *The Advertising Kit* by Jeanette Smith (Lexington Books, 1994). In her book small business advertisers are told they can base their entire plan on answers to questions easily adapted to your break-in plan.

- What impression and effect do you want to make on potential buyers?
- What specific actions must you take to achieve your stated goal and its objectives?
- What timeframe must you build into the plan to accomplish your goal?

Just like a professional plan, yours must do certain things, such as

- Fit your overall strategy
- Translate your goals into measurable and achievable terms
- Develop the specific mix and support strategy that will best meet your objectives
- Create effective monitoring processes to keep your plan on track

## A SKELETAL FRAMEWORK FOR YOUR PLAN

Translating your concepts and your research findings about the product, the customer, and the competition is at the heart of every plan. You've already gathered the bulk of the information you need.

Now it's time to translate the data into an outline for action and accomplishment. To do this, take the following steps:

1. Write down your goal and its objectives. (How to draft goals and objectives is included in Chapter 5.)
2. Describe your strategy.
3. Outline the contents of your presentation.
4. Draft the steps to obtain interviews.
5. Describe the kind(s) of follow-up steps to use after each interview. (Information about "follow up and follow through" is included in Chapter 12.)
6. Determine ways to evaluate results following each interview. This is, in effect, a test of whether you are *communicating* the information you wish to communicate before, during, and after your interview(s).

### Execution!

Now you merely follow the Humpty Dumpty stratagem—put all the pieces together and type them up.

### Not Part of the Plan—But Preparation for Selling YOU

Create an ad! The purpose of the ad is to capture your consumer's attention and include it in your presentation to show your ad-writing skills and abilities.

### Idea

Choose a charity or a cause you care about, and do a *pro bono* example of your area of expertise for that charity or cause. (If you actually give your sample ad to them, they may be able to use it, or at the least, it may stimulate them to solicit funds to run it or find the media that will run it for free.)

**Another Idea**

If you're trying to break into creative, draft an ad setting forth the way you can benefit the agency. It's guaranteed to capture attention and perhaps get across points that when spoken would otherwise sound self-centered and boastful.

In both cases, consider consulting an experienced advertising pro as you draft these ideas. Use this exercise as an opportunity to learn about the creative process by factoring in the feedback of a professional. When you've finished your sample ad, put it aside until you're ready to put your presentation together.

# chapter 9

## Step 5—Put Together a Presentation Package

A presentation package is how an agency shows a would-be client what it can do for them. If putting together a presentation package sounds like work, full-time work it is. But it's worth it to a degree you can never imagine in advance. Take the word of the most successful advertising people in the business—the work you do in advance dictates your success.

This is your chance to talk the talk and walk the walk for the people you want to impress. Your presentation is an opportunity to demonstrate your capabilities and credentials, what you've accomplished, what you've achieved, and what you believe you can contribute to the organization. It's a demonstration of six very important points:

- You love and want to be in the ad business.
- You understand the commitment and dedication that's needed in this business.
- With your ad-client–oriented presentation, you understand the ad business's need for people who grasp the work of pitching clients and doing account reviews.
- You are abreast of new-tech developments that affect advertising.
- You have the smarts, the abilities, and the desire to fit in as a team member and to *add* to the group's success.
- You've done your homework—lots of it—to get a proper feel for this particular potential employer's specialties, its style, and its needs.

If you do your presentation in the style of an agency that's up for review, or one that's trying to land a new account, you'll earn extra points. In other words, a standard resume usually won't cut it in this very unstandard type business.

There's an extra plus when the presentation is patterned for a new business account rather than for an account review. When it's a review, the client sets the rules. When it's for new business, there may be no rules.

In this case, however, this potential client may have some time limits and other minor dictates. But luckily this is the advertising business, and rules can go down the drain if you are able to catch and hold attention. Everyone in this business is constantly looking for people with a passion for it and who have the potential to come up with ideas that are fresh, novel, unique, and creative, that don't necessarily break rules but are refreshingly new. This is your opportunity to demonstrate all that.

## WHAT IS A PRESENTATION?

An advertising presentation is a personal delivery of information, usually supported by both visuals and audio. Orally delivered messages aren't considered as effective as written communication because most people remember things *nonverbally*. But when oral and written are combined, they can be highly productive.

Beyond this, presentations give the presenter immediate feedback, with opportunities for questions to be asked and immediate answers given. There also can be more control over the client's attention to the message you're attempting to get across.

## WHAT IS A PRESENTATION PACKAGE?

A presentation package is several things. For one, it's what you show the client in a face-to-face meeting, which demonstrates what you have to offer. In this case, it's your portfolio, often called your *book* or *spec book*, which is a sampling of your work—or of your ability to do the work. And it also includes your resume, which pins down required but dull facts, figures, and details that can't and shouldn't be included in the actual presentation but are a part of the "leave-behinds."

In fact, preparation of this package should also include a letter that asks for a meeting to precede the presentation. The entire presentation hinges on getting that meeting, so this letter is as important as any part of the presentation package. How to write compelling letters is dealt with in detail in Chapter 12.

In advertising and marketing there are all kinds of presentation packages; the most common are sales presentations and project and new business client presentations. They usually are aimed at more than one person, and they may be presented as informals, semiformals, or formals. They are often elaborate, backed up with visuals and sound, particularly those presented by large agencies.

Yours can—and should—be simple, but it can be just as effective, and it probably will be aimed for one-on-one delivery.

## A Suggestion: Use a Flip Chart

Try using an uncomplicated type of flip chart often used by smaller agencies pitching small businesses. It can be a desktop or a floorstand easel style. You'll use some visuals, but you'll do the audio. When it's less elaborate there's less chance of giving an impression of being mostly flash with little substance.

Keep the presentation format in mind as you write the words for it—a simple succession of headlines backed up with such simplified and dramatized evidence and supporting material as may be required.

These headlines, one to a page, carry the story forward one step at a time. This is a tactic that keeps the prospect from getting ahead of the salesperson, leaping to the wrong conclusion, or skipping some important detail.

## Tips for Writing Headlines

Take the advice of Paula LaRocque, a pro's pro, who is the writing coach/assistant managing editor for one of the nation's leading newspapers, the *Dallas Morning News*. LaRocque discusses the importance of these headings in her column, "Words Matter."

Their import, she says, "is magnified by the fact that even people who don't read the story usually read the headline." They often can serve as the teaser that pulls a scanner to taste the "meat" that follows. Or they can tell a little story about what follows.

"Syntax," says LaRocque, "is crucial to coherent headlines. Subject-verb-object word order is safest." "Words that have more than one meaning can cause 'head' aches," she says. But double meaning, if it lends a little humor, may be the very thing that draws the reader into the words that follow and demonstrates the writer's ability to handle humor, a much desired attribute.

"Every headline writer [at a newspaper] knows how easy it is to make a major gaff. But however challenging it is to write accurate and attractive heads, it is worth the effort," says LaRocque. "That all-important headline is the gateway to the story. If it invites readers, they visit; if it doesn't, readers may stay away." Or, in the case of a presentation, listeners who also have the opportunity to read may tune out what follows the headline.

There will be other writing tips and techniques and suggestions about visuals further on in the chapter.

## Other Suggestions

Go heavy on graphics or visuals only if that is the area you want to break into. Be careful, though, even if that's your dream spot, because there can be visual overload. If art is your strength, use it in your presentation and in discreet ways in your leave-behinds to show your ability.

Actually, before you make a decision about the style and form your presentation will take, ask for a little help. Call upon anyone you know who can tell you about or let you look at professional presentations made by agencies. A college instructor may have some video or print examples. Or contact AAAA (American Association of Advertising Agencies, 666 Third Avenue, New York, New York 10017) for any help they can give you.

Why bother with all this rather than just mail a copy of your resume and portfolio along with a cover letter? There's validation that unsolicited resumes usually end up in a dead-letter bin or are filed away without acknowledgment.

Then why not just offer a written plans book? Because a personal presentation has more force and power. But more importantly, this can be your demonstration of your capabilities and credentials of what you've accomplished, what you've achieved, and what you believe you can contribute to the organization. And it allows an in-person look at your enthusiasm and passion along with an opportunity for the client to ask questions or to get details or clarify something you've purposely kept concise and simple.

It's also a demonstration to show you are abreast of new-tech developments that affect advertising. And it's an opportunity to stress your understanding of the commitment and dedication that's needed in this business.

## A PRESENTATION FOR A NEW PRODUCT

Leo Bogart, an all-time leading advertising strategist, said that consumer goods marketing in a competitive economy depends on a constant infusion of new products. It's equally true that there is constant need for new people to run the ad business. The trick is to make you—as the new product—stand out from competitors and show that you offer substantial, *needed*, and desired benefits for the buyer.

Bogart also pointed out that "a heavy push for a product that no one has ever seen or heard of may tend to create a degree of disbelief, rejection, or resistance." Recognition of a name tends to diminish resistance, he said.

Your challenge then becomes, how can you quickly build a sense of recognition and thereby diminish resistance? That's what you will set out to do with the materials in your presentation package.

## TAKE A LOOK BACK

The first thing to do is go back and take a long look at the product. You did that in Chapter 5 as a personal evaluation. You summed up your attributes, analyzed your strengths and weaknesses, and listed the kinds of contributions you can make to an advertising organization. You also chose the job zone you'd like to be in. All this information is basic to producing your presentation. Organizing it to include only that which is of interest to the potential buyer is the important consideration now.

Also, be sure everything having to do with your presentation includes only positives. Regardless of the business, people want to hire and work with winners—not whiners.

If you're headed for the creative department, your book must include samples. (Of course samples can also be effective for whatever area you're aiming to break into, except perhaps clerical.) Samples? What samples do you have if you haven't yet racked up any on-the-job, hard-core experience?

A very good way to chalk up some sample examples is to volunteer to help out with a nonprofit group's advertising campaign or for an agency's pro bono account. Pro bono advertising? That's free advertising for a charitable cause.

## Samples

If you don't have samples, dream them up. This is where you can really show your creativity and demonstrate that you are able to come up with what is literally the lifeblood of the ad business—ideas. Your samples for creative don't have to be published ads or commercials that have run on radio or television.

But before you slip on your idea cap, let's take a look at ideas and where they come from. Something you may not have realized is that ideas and *research* are bound together. You'd presume the idea always comes first, and sometimes it does. But the final idea comes only after you've checked out all the details surrounding the idea—after you've done your research. Actually, research can be the instigator of ideas.

Three important bits of advice to keep in mind:

1. From Edward Blakeslee: Your most brilliant ideas come in a flash, but the flash comes only after a lot of hard work.

2. From George Grier: It's not at all likely that anyone ever had a totally original idea. He may put together old ideas into a new combination, but the elements that made up the new combination were mostly acquired from other people.

3. And finally, from Andy Rooney: If you can't write it down, you don't have an idea.

Your challenge here is to do some hunting—often called research—to spark ideas for products or services of the type for which the agency you're pitching designs advertising or for products you're familiar with. Or to dream up some ads or commercials for an absolutely nonexistent product or service or for a nonprofit group.

Don't be too glitzy, though. Texans are smart. They come up with sayings that bring home a point and help to keep it in mind, such as "He's all hat and no cattle," for times when glitter outweighs content. Don't let this be said of your ideas.

In today's highly competitive market it seems almost anything goes, and for some advertisers that means using shock treatment to jolt viewers out of their complacency. Remember that a little—a very little—glitter, pizzazz, or any type of shock treatment can go a long way in advertising. They have even less place in your presentation. If your presentation is too glitzy, it may just work to jolt your client to show you the door.

## WHAT THE PROS LOOK FOR—AND DON'T WANT TO SEE

The single most important thing the pros look for is someone who can make immediate and continuing contributions to their group. Thus, the most important thing you must stress is what you can contribute.

Pros also hope to find someone who knows how to break the rules. The best advertising makes you think about the product or service as you've never thought about it before. These are ideas that are adventurous and surprising. As ad pro Ray Champney says, "It takes the expected to unexpected places." Call it imagination and vision.

Something else most pros look for is an ability to get along with others.

What the pros don't want to see is someone who hasn't made adequate preparation for the presentation. This lack says as strongly as if you shout it, this isn't important enough to me to spend the time it takes to put together something worthwhile.

## Some Serious Professional Advice

Garry Marshall is a TV and film producer of some of the funniest comedies around, but his book *Wake Me When It's Funny* (Newmarket Press, 1997), gives outstanding "unfunny" advice about how to "stand out from the crowd." It appeared in *Reader's Digest* in October 1997.

One bit of his guidance is "Never fear failure. Most people try to beat their flaws or deny them altogether. I've always found it best to say [to myself], 'Here are my flaws. Now I have to find something I'm good at.' Don't use your flaws as an excuse to quit." And even when you are embarrassed because you fear you failed, perhaps when your first presentation didn't land the job, Marshall says, "You can't really die of embarrassment. It just *feels* fatal."

## SIX STEPS TO BUILD YOUR SELLING BRIDGE

Newspapers use seven steps for their presentations. Paul Hirt put them into written form for the International Newspaper Promotion Association. Six of them are equally productive for your kind of presentation.

1. Study the sales terrain; learn as much as you can about the specific situation at hand.
2. Creativity: Develop the dramatic idea, which will serve as the title, attention-getter, theme, and continuity device.
3. Start out with a premise with which the prospect must agree.
4. Summarize the benefits at the outset.
5. Develop each benefit with clarity and logic. Relate each back to the title summary.

**6.** Close with a summary that recapitulates the benefits promised at the outset and is proved step-by-step throughout the presentation; ask for the business.

The seventh step, that doesn't apply here, is: Save development of cost and cost comparison until next to closing.

## PUT A PRESENTATION TOGETHER

If this were to be an agency presentation, you wouldn't be going it alone. Agency presentations are always put together and presented by a team. The breaking-in presentation, however, is yours alone.

The one thing every agency strives for is to make presentations that don't follow the crowd, that are different from their competitor's presentations. You, too, must find a way to set yourself apart from your competitors and make yourself memorable—in a dignified, positive way. (The very fact that you're following the ad business's presentation formula may do it for you.)

It will take planning to establish the most convincing approach for your specific audience. You must decide the form or structure in which to present it, and what its content will be, to be sure in advance that it is convincing and substantive. Your presentation must have a grabber opening, persuasive points throughout, and a memorable close. Effective supporting materials also must be chosen or developed to influence opinion and support your contentions about your worth as a member of the organization.

Barbara A. Ganim, in her book *How to Approach an Advertising Agency and Walk Away with the Job You Want* (VGM Career Horizons, 1993), offers a priceless list of twelve Presentation Do's and Don'ts. They're worth studying.

All of this information can pretty much be summed up with one admonition: Put fire in the presentation . . . or vice versa!

### "For Everything You Must Have a Plan"

Napoleon Bonaparte knew what he was saying. But he undoubtedly didn't realize how appropriate his words would remain to this day. Most people don't bother to plan, and for many who do, the plan is something that is just written out—perhaps on assignment— then is either left unfinished or abandoned.

Not this time! The plan you devise will not only show you what to include in the presentation and how to put it together, but it will demonstrate your planning skills. Along with your ideas, these planning skills are what every ad agency looks for in the people it gathers. Ultimately your plan becomes your adviser, for what should and should not be included for this presentation.

## Your Plan Determines the Format

A presentation is often thought of as a talk. Unfortunately, a talk too often becomes a speech that is easy for listeners to tune out. If your objective is to persuade someone that you're the person who should be hired, go light on the talk part and heavy on substance—tangible and visual though concise substance.

Ron Hoff, in his book *I Can See You Naked: A Fearless Guide to Making Great Presentations* (Andrews and McMeel, 1992), probably did the best job of explaining the difference between a speech and a presentation. He wrote:

> **A speech**—a free-wheeling cannon. Creates lots of smoke! Explodes a subject. It takes a subject of some interest and expands it. It is essentially an inside/out operation.

> **A presentation**—a torpedo that speeds precisely to its mark. Starts narrowly and gets sharper. It is essentially an outside/in operation.

There are five parts to this kind of presentation.

- Opening
- Statement of personal goals and how they fit the company's needs
- Samples of what you do

- Testimonials—from people whose word counts
- Close

The mechanics for putting it all together come later.

## The Opening

You've heard people come away from a show or an exhibition shaking their heads about how dull and boring it was. They complain that it was too long, too loaded with technicalities, that it was disorganized. And worst of all—that it didn't address their concerns and interests.

Business presentation authority Terry C. Smith says there's a formula for grabbing attention and holding it all the way through the presentation. In both written and oral form, it follows what he calls the "Tell Them" approach.

He attributes it to an old Southern preacher who, when asked his secret of success for giving such stirring sermons, said: "Easy. I simply tell them what I'm going to tell them. Then I tell them. And then I tell them what I told them."

Smith's comment: "Simple? Yes. Simplistic? *No!*"

Martin Luther King proved the point. He repeated "I have a dream" nine times in 3 minutes, and his words have been remembered for years.

Of course, beyond the formula is the real grabber. What you're going to tell them must be what they want to know.

The opener is there to grab attention and hook your listener(s). It's crucial. It sets the tone and establishes expectations. There's no way to spell out what your opener should be. It depends completely on what your listener is looking for.

One thing should be mentioned here, though—the importance of humor.

## We Interrupt This Message to Bring You an Important Bulletin . . .

Humor works. If you have it, showcase it. As the *New York Times* reported, the "Cliff Freeman & Partners [agency] has managed to turn a toga-clad gnome shouting 'Pizza! Pizza!' and a cast of wacky characters including dancing dogs, feisty grandmothers, and precocious infants into a powerful sales force for the Little Caesars pizza chain."

There's almost universal agreement throughout the advertising industry that if a TV commercial doesn't entertain in its first 10 seconds, it's zapped. There's also agreement that if you can get prospects to laugh, you can get them to buy.

Because humor is essential in the ad business, agency people look hard and long for people who know how to use humor. If you use it in your presentation it may produce extra benefits for you. Your listener won't mentally zap you. He or she will become more receptive to your sales pitch. And you'll greatly heighten your hire perspectives.

Don't panic. You *can* write humor! No less an authority than Bob Hope's joke writer, Gene Perret, said that "everyone can learn to use humor effectively." Your local library has how-to books and articles on the subject. Study a few of them and learn the skill. It could not only put you leagues ahead of your competition and get you hired, it could mean extra paycheck dollars throughout your career.

What's more, you have nothing to lose in attempting humor for your presentation. The worst that can happen is you'll recognize it doesn't quite come off, so you toss the idea and start over in a more straightforward manner. A word of caution: there is nothing worse than humor that isn't funny. Always try it out in advance on associates or friends and watch their reactions.

### Why Humor Works
When Herbert Fried addressed the Adcraft Club of Detroit he explained why humor works so well in advertising.

> We in the business of selling will employ humor, or we'll run the risk of driving consumers to dejection and depression and away from our products and our stores.
> Why do we laugh in the face of tragedy? Fear.
> Bad news scares us because we're human. And

laughing, for one instant, reminds us that things can get better, that life will go on. Humor gives us perspective.

Those words from the head of a product producer add a cautionary note you should remember whether you use humor or not—that buyers must know they're making a *smart decision*. And it's your job to convince your potential buyer with your presentation.

Yes, but you're looking for a job in the uncreative, unfunny job zone of, say, accounting! What place does humor have there?

Well, it's important enough that there's a well-known contest, the Accounting Humor Contest, conducted by the Los Angeles–based accounting firm, the Haller Schwarz agency. Some might question the appropriateness of humor if you are pitching an accounting firm, but this is advertising, and humor is appreciated wherever it raises its funny head.

## Here's the Pitch

Now for the pitch that ties their needs to your goals . . . Actually, you'd better switch that a bit—tie your goals to their needs.

The media call this the "clicker generation." So, presuming you get the listeners past your opener and still have their attention, keep everything that follows tight without being terse. Tell them right off what's in it for them. What you can offer in terms of abilities, skills, and understanding for their type(s) of advertising and clients. Tell them—and *show them*—what you can do. Subtly work in the personal attributes you have to offer, such as a willingness to work long hours and the ability to work with people as a team, or alone, when required.

## Show 'Em You Know 'Em

Some people would call it research—and it is. But your challenge is to offer dead-serious information in a light, interesting manner. You want to let them know you've studied up on them and their clients. The purpose is to show that you seriously want to join their organization because it would satisfy your personal desires to _____. You fill in the blank.

To make the point and its importance, think about a time when someone you barely knew showed that he or she knew something admirable or commendable about you. Just the fact that the person even remembered you plus something about you is gratifying and pleasing. Do it here for the same reasons—to gratify and please. But also do it to show that your desire to join the firm is compelling enough for you to spend serious time and effort checking them out and learning as much as possible about them.

## The Desktop or Easel Presentation

One of advertising's legends, Helmut Krone, makes it sound so simple. "I start with a blank piece of paper and try to fill it with something interesting."

Your assignment here is a little different. It's coming up with headlines, one to a page, that are backed up with copy (*not* meant to fill the page) offering the evidence and supporting material as required.

Paul Hirt makes some vital points about putting presentation copy together. He says, "With so much of the prospect's attention concentrated on the headline, it is vital to make sure that it projects a significant statement," that it's not merely a label, indicating what the page is about. A label head is merely a summary. Your presentation headlines should be significant, affirmative sketches of the supporting evidence on each page.

To make your facts fascinating as you present them in a series of one-to-a-page headlines, often it is helpful to anchor your information to an analogy borrowed from the prospect's own business. That way, Hirt says, you seize the prospect's attention by talking in familiar terms.

## De-junk the Message

Tight editing pays. Words in a presentation should be condensed to the utmost, and don't force your listeners to wade through a flood of words. This simplifies and clarifies the thought and gets it across to a listener.

This means, keep the number of written words to as few as possible so the viewer doesn't have to struggle to read through them. It also means you should keep both your spoken and written messages concise—without being cryptic or terse—so the listener can appreciate the message.

## Graphics and Visuals

There are words. And there are pictures. It's an accepted fact that people remember more of what they see than what they hear. Therefore, whenever possible, convey the message with both words and visuals.

Visuals are used to heighten the clarity of the message and to establish remembrance. Choose them with great discretion and wisdom. If graphic design is the job area you're hoping to join, it's just common sense to design your own visuals to show off your talent.

However, if you can't draw the backside of a cat sitting on a fence, borrow the graphics to dress up your package. If you do this, of course, be sure to spell out loud and clear where you borrowed them from so there's no hint of plagiarism or a feeling that you're attempting to claim a talent you don't have.

## Give 'Em Samples

Now we return to our discussion of samples. If you don't have them, you can prove your capacity for coming up with ideas by dreaming up—manufacturing—some samples.

As a matter of fact, even if you are lucky enough to have had on-the-job training or some rehearsal time working as an intern and you were party to developing a genuine ad, broadcast commercial, direct mail piece, or whatever you can claim as a genuine sample, include some "manufactured" samples along with the genuine articles. This could be doubly beneficial for you. At the same time that it shows you successfully helped produce real advertising, it demonstrates your inventiveness and originality.

## Testimonials

Testimonials are one of the most powerful ad techniques. In the real-life business world they're called recommendations. These can include a letter of recommendation from a college instructor or an ex-boss that attests to a person's character or worth.

In advertising, they're called testimonials or endorsements. And you'd have to have spent your life on another planet not to recognize their power, which is depicted by the number that is used in advertising of every type. Sometimes a celebrity, who is chosen by how well the target buyer relates to him or her, signs on to endorse the product or service. That's called a testimonial campaign. Or the person can be a Mr. or Mrs. Next-Door-Neighbor type, testifying to a truth or fact.

Testimonial sheets also play a big part in advertising. They're collections of quotations from satisfied customers and clients who have good things to say about the product or service. A testimonial sheet is powerful because its numbers mark the depth of approval.

Let's hope you've been collecting these priceless sales stimulators from:

- Instructors who can attest to your diligence, perseverance and persistence, as well as your understanding of the industry.
- Business people who know your work ethics.
- Celebrities whose words will likely impress your potential customer. Yes, celebrities—ad business celebrities! They don't have to be famous, but the impact of their recommendations is much greater if they are connected in one way or another to advertising.

Testimonials can work for your presentation if the names and words are likely to hit home with the listener. Build two or three of the best into your flip chart, but make the typeface and size easily readable from a distance so your audience can read them instead of you reading them to the audience. That saves any discomfort for you or a misleading look of conceit on your part.

In addition to using your testimonial in your presentation, you should make up a testimonial sheet to include as part of your leave-behinds, to be read at the recipients' leisure. If you use a testimonial sheet, do as advertisers do—be sure your name, address, and phone number appears on the sheet. A good place to list this is below the last testimonial.

## A Testimonial Collector for Life

If you don't already have a collection of testimonials, start seeking them out immediately. And keep collecting them throughout your career.

Send out letters requesting them. The example in Exhibit 9.1 is adapted from a sample letter Robert W. Bly offers in his book *Advertising Manager's Handbook* (Prentice-Hall). Bly calls attention to the fact that in his sample letter, the writer asks for an "opinion" instead of a testimonial and that it solicits criticisms as well as positive comments. In this way, he tells his readers, "you are not just requesting a favor; you are getting information that will help you serve your clients or customers better in the future. Thus, you both profit from the exchange."

## Now for the Close

It's pretty much accepted these days that television has caused people to have short attention spans. There's evidence that people pay more attention at the beginning and the end of a presentation. That's because, the authorities tell us, at the start they want to know what you're going to say, and at the end they want to hear the closing information.

If you follow the preacher's earlier advice, now's the time to tell them what you've told them. Call it a summary of the most important points.

If you've used humor at the beginning, now may be an excellent time to add another dab of it. It will leave your listener(s) feeling good.

Mr. John Smith
ABC Co.
Anytown, USA

Dear John:

I have a favor to ask of you.

I'm in the process of putting together a presentation and some leave-behinds to use in my search for a job with an advertising agency.

I plan to include a testimonial sheet—a collection of comments about my knowledge of and love for the advertising business, my work ethics, and my abilities and skills.

Would you please take a few minutes to give your opinion of my competence and aptitude.

There's no need to dictate a letter—just jot your comments on the back of this letter, sign below, and return to me in the enclosed envelope. The second copy is for your files.

I look forward to learning what you think about my capability to be of assistance and benefit to a future employer. I welcome any suggestions or criticism, too.

Many thanks, John.

Sincerely,


Betty Jones


BETTY: YOU HAVE MY PERMISSION TO QUOTE FROM MY COMMENTS AND USE THESE QUOTATIONS IN PRESENTATIONS, A TESTIMONIAL SHEET, IN ADS, BROCHURES, MAIL, AND OTHER PROMOTIONS USED TO SECURE A JOB IN ADVERTISING OR TO MARKET YOUR SERVICES.

Signed_____ Date_____

**Exhibit 9.1**

Or you could close with one of your ideas that you saved until last, as a reminder that you're full of ideas. The most effective idea would be one that would work for the customer. This adds a bit more excitement or drama to the close.

Whatever you close with, be sure it's something that will be remembered tomorrow—and next week. A good close might be to repeat an idea or strategy you offered earlier in the presentation.

There's research that shows that the last person interviewed for a job is the most likely person to get the job. If you're not lucky enough to be last, at least try to be memorable. And build your leave-behinds to renew and restore their remembrance of you.

## LEAVE-BEHINDS SHOULD NOT BE THROWAWAYS

Leave-behinds are like your calling card. Only they say a lot more about you than a calling card.

Nothing was more important than your presentation—until you finished presenting it. No matter how impressive it was, you and it may not be remembered past the next person's presentation. And being remembered—*positively*—is the secret to being called back for another talk or to talk about being hired.

The purpose of your leave-behinds is so that days later, the client will distinctly remember *you* and your presentation, and separate you from the blur of the other applicants.

After most major professional presentations, agencies leave a written document called a *plansbook*. It's a well-organized companion piece that puts what the presentation has offered in writing. It's prepared at the same time as the presentation and is to be used as a reference. An agency's plansbook is far more detailed than its presentation, but it's designed to look like the presentation. It's meant to be a reflection of the kind and style of work the agency proposes for the client.

Plansbooks are made to show the client that this agency stands out from the competition. That's the objective for your leave-behind packet—to show and *remind* that you do stand out from the competition, and they can benefit from hiring you.

Sometimes agencies also leave a specially prepared audiotape or videotape that sums up everything they want the possible client to remember and consider.

These planbooks and tapes are far too elaborate for your use. A much less expensive leave-behind packet should do the trick for you if it contains the kinds of information that the people you're aiming to impress feel is worth keeping. Prepare your leave-behind in the format of a press kit. It should include

- A resume
- Samples as you presented them of actual advertising or of manufactured ads you dreamed up
- A copy of your testimonial sheet or copies of impressive letters of recommendation from people whose names and titles are tied to the industry and whose endorsement thus is noteworthy
- Most important—and in the most visible spot—your name and where you can be reached, or a business card. Add a Rolodex-type card, filled out with name, address, and telephone number with fax and e-mail numbers if you have them.

## YOUR RESUME

Remember, your resume is not an autobiography or a memoir! It's really a promotion piece, an image marketing piece about *you*. Its primary purpose is to convince potential buyers that you have what they want *and need*. It should be written to keep the memory of you alive past however many other presenters follow you.

First, go around to the other side of that desk—in your imagination, of course—and look at what the person you're preparing the resume for wants to know about you. Look also at your competition, and build it to lessen the attractiveness of their advantages and benefits and make yours more appealing.

And do it all in 250 words or less!

The trick is to make this message about your skills, experience, and accomplishments come alive in a totally positive manner that entices interest and encourages remembrance. Just because it's called a resume doesn't mean you must use the deadly dull format of standard resumes. Remember, this is advertising—for *you!*

There's a reason for you to keep your resume concise. Companies now have computer software that cuts resumes they have received to only two or three lines of the most pertinent information. If yours is too long, you can count on its being software-edited to size—their size—or away entirely.

For those inclined to include personal interests: Don't! Not unless in some way a hobby or other personal interest reinforces your qualifications. If, for instance, the agency specializes in sports advertising then your sports knowledge and participation *could* have merit. Sort it out carefully, however.

## Don't Use a Resume to Solicit a Job

*Knight-Ridder/Tribune Business News* had some excellent advice for job seekers. It headlined the article "Unsolicited Resumes Rarely Find a Job." That alone is worth the price of a copy of the newspaper. But the article gave more practical advice.

"Amplify your good points," it says "de-emphasize weaker areas and don't wear a false face anywhere but at a masquerade."

## "Keep the NOUN in this AnNOUNcement"

Let's return to the computer software that sorts out sought-after information from scanned e-mail resumes as well as postal versions.

It's usually done by a search for specific nouns—key descriptors of qualifications. Employment adviser Joyce Lain Kennedy, in her "Sun Features" column in the *Dallas Morning News*, describes how it works:

> Power words on a paper resume tend to be action verbs and such adjectives and adverbs as "aggressive," "responsible" and "hard-working." [These types of words are] not being scanned or recognized anymore.

> Computers, heartless machines that they are, don't care a whit about your sterling character. When computers screen for applicants, they want 'just the facts, ma'am.' And those facts are usually nouns.

It's Kennedy who uses a cartoon drawing by Eddie Eddings in her column to caution readers to "Remember To Keep the NOUN in [Your] AnNOUNcement!"

## PUT YOUR BEST FEAT FORWARD

The right skills get you in the door. But how do you know in the beginning which are the right ones to show in your resume?

Check out the sought-after skills mentioned in job ads in *Advertising Age* or *Adweek*. Also, there are Internet sites such as the one that lists "Important Job Skills for California's Top Fifty Occupations."

Also of value is an institutional software program called "SkillsUP" (www.skillsup.com). The company that developed it, UP Software, says that the first part shows you how skills are used in each of 250 occupations; the second part steps you through a personal skills improvement plan.

Jim Hurd, the CEO of the company that created the SkillsUP software, says he sees "a beefy and well-articulated skills package as better than money in the bank. We track our financial assets," he says, "on a weekly and monthly basis, but almost none of us understands how to track and strengthen our skills assets, which are the most important money-earning capital we possess. And remember, you may lose your money, but you won't lose your skills."

There are other software programs that connect skills to jobs. Check your library, colleges, and job and career centers.

As you search, you may come across terms such as "success factors." They're merely attempts to give a new name to the age-old, time-worn word, "skills." There's often a problem in gathering a list of your skills. We seldom fully recognize our own talents and abilities. They're so much a part of us that we just don't recognize them or their value.

If you're short on the skills needed in the ad business, they can be learned. That means, as you travel your career road, your skills can be updated, moved around, or new ones learned to fill needs.

# chapter 10

## Step 6—Make the Presentation and Capture the Job

There's a lot to be *re*-said here, such as "to put yourself in their position—try on their shoes." A successful presenter did that—literally! Just before he made his presentation, he pulled out a pair of the biggest shoes he could find. When he put them on he looked like a 4-year-old playing grown-up, wearing Daddy's shoes.

Everyone in the room grinned, but the presenter kept an absolutely straight face as he stood up, looked directly at the top executive, and said, "I just want to try and see what it feels like to be in your shoes—wearing the biggest shoes in the ad agency business in this town—and needing to hire a new person to lessen the workload a little."

The importance of a presentation bears repeating, too. Ron Hoff, a presentation consultant, reduces it to a sentence: "Presentations? That's how we in advertising win our business—how we keep our business—and how we lose our business."

This is where the agency pitches the product and captures the client. This is also the time when you can win your business, or lose it. And if you win it, the strength of your presentation could very well help you to become a future member of the agency's presentation team.

In the advertising business, presentations have become indispensable—and Hoff attributes it to television. "We are so used to *watching* people talk to us on TV . . . to *see* the people . . . see how they think, how they handle themselves under pressure. We want to sense the interaction of a 'live' presentation. We want to feel the chemistry." No one has ever figured out how many dollars the ad business spends on presentations every year, but Hoff says *Business Week* estimated that U.S. business conducts more than 33 million presentations every business day. Then this top authority in the field gives advice worth tattooing on your forehead: "If you want to make it big in advertising (or any business)," he says, "you'd better put 'presentations' somewhere near the top of your list of required courses."

It's easy to say that your presentation is absolutely the most important part of breaking into advertising—because it is. But if what goes into it isn't super-researched, super-thought-out in advance, it won't accomplish much of anything. You'd do just as well walking in without a thing in hand—or in head!

## DRESS REHEARSALS

If this were to be a presentation by an agency, it would call for team rehearsals. In this instance you'll go it alone, but it calls for as many practice sessions as necessary to reach a point where you know your content well enough to be completely comfortable with it. Ron Hoff suggests at least ten rehearsals.

That's a secret of overcoming fear and extreme nervousness— knowing the content so completely that it's like talking to a friend about an experience you've had. And knowing it so completely that if for any reason there's a hitch in the tangibles, you know the message well enough not to be distracted and can continue through to the end.

A certain degree of nervousness is acceptable, and it's also expected by those listening and watching. Just don't let it show to the point it makes *them* nervous and you uncomfortable.

### Voice Language Can Say a Lot

A good way to practice alone is with a tape recorder. Each time you do a recording, replay it to pick up bumbling, sloppy spots, areas where you need more practice, or where there is a need for content revision.

But what tape recorders do best is let you hear yourself as others hear you. Some people just have voices that grate. They're too high, too nasal, too loud, too mumbly, or they speak too fast.

All of these qualities or traits can be changed when you become conscious that they exist. This is not an admonition to speak in a monotone. A range in voice pitch is natural and definitely desirable. Just be sure it doesn't reach such a high pitch that listening ears block out this unpleasant sound.

It's necessary to speak loudly enough to be easily and comfortably heard. There is a problem, however, if nervousness tends to increase one's voice volume and the person sounds like he or she is shouting.

In her book *Say It With Confidence* (Warner Books, 1997), Margo T. Krasne gives excellent advice. She says confidence "comes from three things and three things only: (1) knowing what to do, (2) learning how to do it, and (3) doing it often enough so you can do it with confidence." Negative, and positive, voice characteristics show up loud and clear as you replay audio tapings.

Tape recorders don't show body language, however. After you've perfected the oral part, try to do some videotapings.

## Listen to Your Body Language

Everyone's body talks. What does *yours* say? Does it cancel the words that come out of your mouth? Videotaping will give you a pretty good idea about whether your body language is yelling something so loudly that it's drowning out the words you want your listener to hear.

Incidentally, experts tell us that the right body language makes your words more effective, while the wrong body-speak can scramble the message.

Psychiatrists and speaking coaches tell us that when there's a discrepancy between what a person says and what that person's body tells us, that we should believe what we see, not what we hear. Because, they say, while words can be manipulated, gestures are a lot harder to control. They're harder to control unless we can see ourselves saying the words. A friend can tell you what your body is doing, but it's so much easier to understand its impact when you can see it for yourself, on tape.

There's one particular stance to avoid no matter what. When you stand with arms folded across your chest it virtually shouts resistance on your part, and viewers may not realize how much they, in turn, are resisting you and what you're telling them. If you're standing, keep your arms loosely at your sides to give a more receptive attitude. And if you're sitting, lean forward a little—it conveys an amiable impression.

Eye contact is the most remembered element in forming an impression. Look people in the eye for 3 or 4 seconds, but don't stare.

## DECODE TORSO TALK

It was an anthropologist who helped decipher body language. Ray L. Birdwhistell is best remembered for his research in the field of nonverbal communication, now called *body language*. He, with his colleagues, put forth the idea in the '40s that body motions constituted a code that could be cracked. Birdwhistell cracked the code by working out a system of transcription for body movements using slow-motion movie footage showing people talking, and then he trained people in using that system.

One of his colleagues said, "He could show how to communicate emphasis with the raising of an eyebrow or the flip of a finger or the tap of a toe." But when Birdwhistell was interviewed in 1970 he said, "There are no universal gestures. As far as we know, there is no single facial expression, stance, or body position that conveys the same meaning in all societies."

## KEEP PRACTICING!

Don't get discouraged if it takes a number of trial runs to come up with polished content that is well remembered and rehearsed so it doesn't sound memorized or overly rehearsed. Remember, this is a talk, a conversation—not a speech. There should be no indication that anything has been memorized.

People "fail to realize how much of their success is dependent on the way they speak. Poor speaking habits can destroy credibility," says Ty Boyd in an *Entrepreneur* magazine article. The author of *The Sales Bible* says, "Most people don't realize how weak their presentation skills really are—and how easy it is to reverse the process if they just focus on the fundamentals." His success tactics for salespeople can be adapted to your purposes. They include:

- Get a feel for timing. One of the biggest mistakes salespeople make is going too fast.
- Read a chapter from a sales book aloud, recording it on audiotape. Play it in your car. You'll learn about presentations and about how you present your pitch.
- Videotape your opening 5 minutes. Ask a friend or colleague to be the prospect and rate your performance.
- Be your own video critic once a week. Watch the tape at home; correct your two worst habits and enhance your two best strengths.
- Be prepared. Have your product down cold.
- Be yourself. Being genuine will win the prospect's confidence (and the sale).

When anyone tells you, "It's not what you say, it's how you say it," tell them as *Entrepreneur* magazine suggests, "You're *wrong!*" It's definitely *what* you say—as well as *how* you say it!

These trial runs are not dress rehearsals, however. A dress rehearsal is really only putting on the clothes you'll wear and getting comfortable wearing them.

## Their Bodies Talk, Too

Don't be clueless in the meeting. If you know the language, you can spot danger signals.

Don E. Schultz, in his book *Strategic Advertising Campaigns* (National Textbook Company, 1990), tells us that "people may lie, but body language never does." And he also says not to read a lot of significance into isolated signals of body language among those in your audience.

If a member of your audience is sitting there with his fingers interlaced across his belly, it doesn't always mean that he is putting up a barrier to your message. This may be the customary meeting posture of this particular person.

But if the fingers are interlaced, the legs are crossed, the person has slithered down into his or her seat and is looking out the window—it's safe to say that you've got a problem. The body language, en toto, is issuing a stern rejection of your message. You've got to do something. Anything. You may want to get him or her involved in a bit of Q&A, or call a break, or call for an audible. "Change" is the immediate and obvious answer.

You'll know you're losing them when you spot them looking at their watches or when you catch them yawning.

Other clues that tell you how the audience is responding include:

- Coughing. That indicates nervousness and a reaction of how-much-longer-is-this-going-to-take? on their part.
- Note taking. A good sign—that what you're saying is worth remembering.
- Wandering eyes. An indication of boredom.
- Surreptitious reading. If it's not material you've given them, *do something quickly!*

## A Few Tricks to Get Attention Back

- Pause. "Dead air" catches everyone's attention, which is evident when you're listening to TV or radio and there's a sudden pause. If your attention has wandered, it comes back fast. "What's the matter?" you wonder. But keep your pause just short enough to grab their attention.
- Move about. Get away from the podium or lectern or whatever you've been standing motionless behind. Get closer to your audience and remind them that you're alive and well and enjoying this time with them.

- Be more animated, more entertaining.
- Involve the audience. Ask a question. Or ask for an opinion.

## WHO'S WATCHING—AND WHO'S PAYING ATTENTION?

There's scientific research that is valuable in helping you make decisions about the visuals you choose for your presentation. The research also proves the necessity to keep visual elements in the presentation simple—even in this time of TV visual overload.

In 1984 advertising icon Leo Bogart stated unequivocally in his book *Strategy in Advertising* (NTC Business Books) that novelty and complexity attract our attention. However, he also says there is a distinction between "looking" and "attending," which, of course, is important in getting your verbal and visual messages across.

When people look at pictures they tend to concentrate on a small part of the total area (usually less than 10 percent). So the amount of information acquired from a picture depends on the number of separate fixations and not on how long they last.

Bogart quotes psychologist Norman Mackworth, who says that because pictures represent more complex visual phenomena than words, pictorial information is processed more slowly than words. To translate this into advice for your presentation, it comes down to "keep your visuals simple, too."

As for the question of who's paying attention, that comes down to planned control of your audience. Remember, this is a conversation, not a speech. And a conversation is interactive, so your presentation must be interactive, too. You can keep attention focused because you are using the right arrows. You know exactly *who* your target is. You know what the agency's needs and wants are. You offer benefits they need and ones that, hopefully, they can't resist.

## HERE'S WHAT YOUR AUDIENCE LOOKS FOR

Regardless of the job zone, agency representatives look for a presentation that is neat, well organized, well designed, and well thought out.

A creative director probably adds the stipulation that it must be innovative and "visually pleasing." He or she is undoubtedly looking for the presentation to display creative ideas. As one director said, "I look for a presentation that expresses an idea in simple, compelling words and pictures."

Agency people want to see a presentation that breaks rules, that "takes the expected to unexpected places," as one executive explained it. You can be sure that anyone you are making a presentation to has seen enough of them to be able to get a good sense of your personal feelings. If you present yours in a way that shows you're genuinely proud of it, and if you convey enjoyment, enthusiasm, and excitement, you'll undoubtedly come across as someone who loves the ad business. Everyone in the business looks for these traits.

On-the-job training is rare these days: it's too costly and takes too long for the person to become a contributor. So you can be sure the people you present to are looking for someone who can start work the day they arrive at work, who can make immediate and ongoing contributions, and whose contributions justify the salary.

Barbara A. Ganim says in her very helpful book, *How to Approach an Advertising Agency and Walk Away With the Job You Want* (VGM Career Horizons, 1993), that there are certain job search mistakes most people make. They are:

- Failing to target specific agencies
- Not knowing what *you* really want and which agency is best suited to you
- Not grabbing attention with initial contact
- Not understanding how advertising *really* works
- Relying on want ads
- Not being prepared for the interview

(We said early on, there'd be a lot to be *re*-said in this chapter. Re-saying it reminds, and some things are so important they can't be said too often.)

## THE CURTAIN IS ABOUT TO RISE

You've made the difficult decisions about whether the presentation is to be formal or informal. About whether its tone reflects the image of the agency you're pitching, the agency you're hoping to join. You've chosen the points that make you distinctive and that match first, the agency's needs, and second, their wants about the person they bring aboard. And you've settled on the image you want to project, to convey your demeanor as a "fit" with the agency's image.

Most presentations made by agencies are upbeat but serious in a relaxed, enthusiastic, and friendly way. The presenters have had enough previous experience to be able to appear relaxed and self-confident, to sense audience reaction, and change anything that brings a negative or bored response.

You may not be quite that expert yet, and it's not expected of you. But try your best to be relaxed, enthusiastic and friendly. Remember that each time you make a presentation you're improving your ability and coming closer to the professionalism agency people acquire.

Perhaps you could tickle your funnybone a bit by remembering a Wise and Aldrich cartoon. It shows a guy who hasn't bothered to shave for days, who says, "We're in the last rounds of presentations, and for good luck, I'm not shaving until we win the account." Remember, as you face your audience, it's almost as hard on them as on you.

## FIT TO BE EYED?

You're the product, so your packaging is important. In advertising, packaging can mean the difference between success or failure at the point of purchase.

The lead to an article in *Business Start-Ups* rounds up just about where you are. It says, "You've developed a prototype, worked out all the bugs in your invention and even found a manufacturer. Are you ready to roll? Not yet. There's still one crucial component of success you need to work on: packaging."

For the packaging of Classico pasta sauces, shape and graphics work together to make a powerful pitch. It's sold in a mason jar, which suggests homemade. And the label, with its landscapes and depictions of ingredients, sends another message, according to Thomas Hine, author of *The Total Package: The Evolution and Secret Meanings of Boxes, Bottles, Cans and Tubes* (Little Brown, 1995). "It's flattering to the buyers: 'We know you've traveled, and we know you don't buy industrial tomato sauce, that you're a more discriminating buyer and are willing to pay a price of about 40 to 50 percent more than Ragu.'"

A letter from a reader to *Brandweek* said, "The package *is* the product. Consumers won't admit in any kind of poll that they are greatly influenced by packaging, but they are. And most of the time, they're *negatively* affected." The writer suggested that advertisers should carve that into their desks. It also bears remembering concerning your look as you look for a job.

Take the example that follows as a never, never—no matter how relaxed an impression you wish to give. It was a letter asking for advice, written by a reader of *Editor & Publisher* magazine. It said, "I'm a manager looking to change companies. A few years ago I got an earring that has become part of 'my look.' My wife argues that I should take it out for job interviews, but I say that if an employer doesn't want a stylish guy, I might as well know up front. What do you fellas think?"

The sum of the answer was short but not very sweet. "I can't believe that anyone would choose to limit his career for the sake of an earring. It's just plain dumb." The *E&P* writer also acknowledged that "what's just plain dumb is that anyone would care if a male employee wears an earring. But the fact is that most do."

Good advice. *After* the job is pinned down, then the new member of the crew can look around at what other members are wearing and decide if an offbeat look is worth fighting for. The final bit of advice from *E&P* was, "Employers are impressed by employees willing to work at impressing their employers."

Suitable dress for making a presentation depends on the physical circumstances at the agency and the type of presentation you'll be making. If it's in the board room or a conference room with several people attending, a suit is appropriate. If it's in the executive's office, a sports jacket with or without tie may be just fine. Try and check in advance about the kind of meeting this will be.

Your appearance is important in creating that first impression. If everyone is wearing jeans, you may want to take the sports jacket approach. If suits and ties are the order for the agency people, a suit and tie is appropriate for a male presenter and nothing too flashy or too offbeat for a woman—no frilly dresses or low-cut necklines.

Just be sure you're comfortable in whatever you choose to wear or you'll unconsciously tug and pull and not only distract your listeners but divert your own concentration.

## IT'S SHOW AND TELL TIME

Making a presentation by an advertising agency usually includes setting up the room. In this case, maybe not.

There probably will be no opportunity to set up the room. You may not even know where your presentation will be made. It may be in the most informal of surroundings, in a private office, or in a small conference room, where it's strictly one-to-one with little room for equipment. Most conference rooms and top executives' offices have conference tables, where you could set up your tabletop flip-top easel. If you don't know the confines of the place where you'll make your presentation, don't count on having access to a table. Go for a floorstand easel.

Also, go for the simplest of equipment. A slide projector is out unless you know there'll be a screen on which to show the visuals. Or that you can somehow use a blank page of your floorstand easel as a screen and that the page or projector won't have to be tilted, resulting in distorted images.

An overhead projector is easy to use, but it means lugging it, along with your flip-top equipment, and that may present a problem you can't afford to face.

Visuals in addition to your flip pages are excellent additions to an otherwise strictly verbal demonstration. They can be proof of what you're saying and a demonstration of an idea or a thought. But, as the pros know, learning to master their use is the most difficult part of the entire procedure. If you use visuals that require equipment, practice until you're completely comfortable using it and know how to hook it up fast. And know what to do if it suddenly goes out on you.

There may be other props to deal with. If there's anything that's a semblance of a lectern, stay away from it. A lectern accomplishes the same objective as crossing your arms over your chest—it separates you from your audience and denies that this is a friendly conversational type of meeting.

Don't use notes. Practice has made you confident of what you'll say and do, and each page of the easel presentation is a reminder of what to say at that specific point.

Forget pointers, too. This is an informal *talk*, not a speech, with tables of numbers or schematics.

## THE SHOW IS READY; IT'S TELL TIME

The first 5 minutes of your presentation are critical. Actually, you must capture attention immediately, but you're ready for that with the opening "grabber" you decided on when you put the presentation material together.

All you need to do now is take a deep breath, relax your shoulders (which may be hunched up around your ears, if you're overly nervous), and go for it. If it turns out to do what you want it to do, that's a dream come true. If it doesn't, you're lucky! It can be a better practice than you can ever get back home before your make-believe audience. And it can give you a hard-core indication of ways you can change certain things for a better acceptance and response.

## Interactive—Buzzword of Advertising

A Q&A period is as much a part of a presentation as creative is in the ad business. With Q&A it's all interactive. Questions are an excellent indicator of interest. No questions. Little interest. Questions also tell you where the interest lies—and whether you did an adequate amount of homework to spark that interest.

A good way to start off a Q&A session—and avoid that dead-air period when no one is quite ready with a question—is with a question of your own. Be prepared with a pleasant question directed to the executive or one of those sitting in on the meeting.

Questions can sometimes be difficult and loaded. It helps to plan for the Q&A session just as you planned your presentation, to be able to anticipate questions, and to be ready with some answers. Earlier, while you have your buddies assembled to critique your presentation, you can ask them to dream up questions and to ask the most difficult ones they can think of.

The questions inevitably will be about you, so ask your practice audience to dream up dumb and potentially embarrassing ones, because those are the ones you may not anticipate on your own. Try to depersonalize your answers, perhaps by pinpointing something in the question(s) that relate to your presentation or the message within the presentation.

Ron Fry, in his book *101 Great Answers to the Toughest Interview Questions* (Career Press, 1996), says there are three killer questions:

1. So, tell me about yourself.
2. Have you ever been fired?
3. What are your salary requirements?

If you don't have ready answers for these, get hold of a copy of Fry's book so you can "Prepare to be Prepared," as he puts it.

Recognize that sometimes difficult or loaded questions are asked merely to see how you handle them, rather than for the answer you'll give. No matter how difficult the question, remember to think before you answer. Avoid long explanations that inevitably turn into dumb answers. If a question elevates your dander, instead of trying to answer it immediately, play for a little cool-down time by asking the person to rephrase it.

There's an absolute must—answer all questions affably and graciously. A good thing to know is that seemingly hostile or loaded questions usually put the rest of the audience on the side of the person being questioned.

Also, just as with the rest of your presentation, you should practice and rehearse.

## Listen Up!

Too often, the people asking the questions don't bother to pay much attention to the answers. In this case, you must listen to what people's questions are *saying*. They'll clue you to what their interests are and to what's important to *them*.

There's a listening technique that was first introduced twenty-five years ago. It's called NLP—neuro-linguistic programming—and just as its name indicates, it's complex and sometimes difficult to understand. According to John Emerick Jr., author of *Be the Person You Want to Be: Harness the Power of Neuro-Linguistic Programming to Reach Your Potential* (Prima Publications, 1997), its promise is to help people improve their harmony and understanding with others.

When *Entrepreneur* first reported on the concept, the magazine said, "NLP teaches trainees to recognize and understand body language, including eye movements, nonverbal communication such as vocal rhythm and tone, and key words that carry extra meaning. NLP's central premise is that people are programmed to think, act, and feel by their thoughts, beliefs, feelings, language, and behavior. The idea is that identifying and changing these influences can make us more effective both personally and professionally."

The title of Emerick's book makes it sound so easy. It's clearly a complex issue, but there are numerous books, videotapes, and audiotapes explaining it. If your time and your interest in the subject is sufficient, you may want to take a look at this method of bonding with individuals and audiences.

At least, follow Lyndon Johnson's advice during their part of your Q&A session: "Be quiet. You ain't learning when you're talking."

## STOP THE Q&A AND DO A ROUNDUP

So often when the Q&A runs out of steam, the presenter just sits down. Thus ends the presentation.

Don't let this happen. When questions wind down, call a halt and then do a brief roundup. It's important—essential—that you leave your audience remembering you, not the last question or questioner.

You want to leave them remembering you and your ideas. To do this, reinforce what you told them earlier—that you've taken time to learn all you could about them, their clients, and their specialties. Restate how this research tells you that your abilities, talents, and skills fit their needs.

As you're ready to walk out the door, pick up your packet of leave-behinds and hand it to the appropriate person—the person you'll be in contact with later. Leave-behinds are meant to act as a reminder—of you, your talents and skills, and the benefits you can bring to their organization.

Make your entire roundup as *concise* as possible. And . . .

## KNOW WHEN TO LEAVE

No one can advise you as to when it's time for you to leave any specific meeting. But surely you can get a feeling for when it's a good time to leave or when you've overstayed your welcome.

It's always best to "leave them hungry," as some agency people say. Leave them wanting to know more. This doesn't mean an abrupt departure that might indicate you can't wait to get out of there. Rather, say something about how glad you are you had the opportunity to talk to them and that you'll be in touch.

## STAY IN TOUCH

Unless yours was the presentation to end all presentations, you didn't hear the magic words "You're hired!" before you left.

Undoubtedly there are others competing for a place with the same agency, and although your presentation may have been the best offered, the hackneyed phrase "Out of sight, out of mind" becomes the doctrine of their day. Your leave-behinds were probably given to a secretary and filed "for future reference." They certainly weren't put on an easel on the boss's desk as a reminder of the great job you did. This was, after all, a get-acquainted meeting. At this stage in the game, there's really only one way to remain remembered—*stay in touch*.

That means a telephone call now and then, perhaps once every ten days or two weeks. A good way to know how often you should call is to ask, "Is it okay if I call you in a couple of weeks to check in with you?"

Once you've placed this call, make the rest of your follow-up calls to the contacts you've gathered. Let them know you're still ready, willing, and very able. Just as are agency people to whom you've made a presentation, these are busy people. They may want to help, but for them once you're out of sight you're also out of mind. Keep nudging, gently.

# chapter 11

## Reaching Out to New-Tech Advertising

Nowhere is the warning more evident about how fast everything is changing than a Lucent TV commercial, as the churchly voice-over tells the audience: "Dearly Beloved, we are gathered here to pay our last respects to the Internet as we know it."

The Internet "as we know it," *dead?* Who can believe that?

Not too many years ago the status quo was to use mainstream media for advertising, but now the Web is becoming a mainstream medium and changing as fast as it is gathering followers. One of the biggest success stories comes from Toyota, a pioneer in Web advertising. "During the twelve months ending in May [1997], the Toyota Web site received more than 152,000 requests for product brochures," *Business Week* reported. Far more important is that a comparison of actual sales of cars against the names of those who requested the brochures showed that the Web ad campaign was directly responsible for the sale of 7,329 cars.

## THE "GRAY LADY" GOES NEW-TECH

One of the greatest indications of the impact of new-tech is that even the cautious and careful *New York Times* has boarded the bus. Now it not only publishes in color, but in February 1998 it extended its Thursday print editions to include a weekly special section called "Circuits." In its first 20-page issue, it told readers that it was "expanding coverage of the kind of technology that has already changed the lives of everyone who uses a computer or a cellular phone, everyone who uses a credit card or drives a car, everyone who has a Social Security number—anything with a chip in it."

Shortly after "Circuits" was introduced, *Advertising Age* reported a Forrester study that shows users are ready for e-commerce. "By the end of [1998], 50 percent of North American households will own PCs, up from 43 percent in 1997, and 29 percent will have an online connection." The study also revealed that "while only 5 percent of North Americans now make purchases online, 10 percent will conduct transactions over the Internet by [the end of 1997]."

The good news is consumers undoubtedly recognized the Web's importance, seeing how far the *Times* is taking its recognition of the public's interest in new-tech developments and its belief in the future of cyber-advertising. The section even has its own online address: Circuits@nytimes.com.

The bad news is "Many ad agencies lack knowledge and expertise about advertising online—and are treating online advertising as a fad," *Adweek* reported in its Eastern Edition.

All this means the need for cyber-savvy mortals is nearing crisis level. And it means everyone expecting to work in any form of communications, especially in advertising, must be Net-literate as well as "byte-bonded" (understanding computer use).

What is also impressive, particularly for those planning a career in advertising and who have this kind of new-tech knowledge, are the predictions for spending in cyberspace.

*Advertising Age* reported that $906.5 million was spent on Web advertising in 1997—more than three times the amount spent in 1996—and predicts it will reach $4.3 billion by 2000. Internet spending is growing faster than traditional media, the report stated, and although "it is still at the bottom of the heap in terms of ad dollars generated, it's closing in on outdoor advertising revenue, which totaled $1.4 billion in 1997."

"Internet commerce will grow at a breakneck pace over the next five years," according to Forrester Research, Inc. It predicts the value of products and services traded between companies will grow from $8 billion in 1997 to $327 billion in 2002.

So what's the importance of this kind of information? It tells you that you'd better not just get yourself acquainted with this new-tech medium, but you must stay abreast of it if you plan to break into or to stick around anywhere in the advertising game.

## Other Media Feeling the Impact

A tracking survey by IntelliQuest showed that TV is feeling the greatest impact from the growth of technology. "Twenty-six percent of Internet users watch less TV."

Print reading—of newspapers, magazines, and books—interestingly, fares better, with only 10 percent saying they do less reading because of their Internet use. Another research group, Cyber Dialogue, reports even higher numbers. Their research shows that 35 percent of Net users watch less TV and 16 percent read less.

Seymour Topping, director of editorial development for New York Times, Co., attributed a falloff of 26 percent in their advertising to the fact that "newspapers used to reach 80 percent of U.S. households; their penetration has dropped to 67 percent."

Cyber Dialogue also found two more interesting facts. Long-distance phone calls fell by 22 percent. Radio, however, is affected the least, probably because "many Internet users listen to the radio while surfing the Web or checking e-mail," they speculate.

The bottom line is that in 1997 there were more than 24 million Americans using the Web. That's an audience which, according to advertising authorities, is too large to be ignored and one that mainstream consumer corporations as well as the nation's largest advertising agencies have finally come to recognize is a surprisingly effective avenue they must consider in order to reach American consumers. And they're doing it, reports *Business Week* magazine.

## Interactive Newspapers

It's not only advertising agencies that need cyber-savvy employees, newspapers need them, too, because the news business is no longer what it used to be. As Ziggy moans in a Tom Wilson cartoon, "What's the world coming to? Now my paperboy won't even make house calls!"

Nope. Newspaper boys are out of business, and delivery of the news—and print ads—is via the Net. Well, not completely. But the numbers and strength of online newspapers is increasing every year. And it's not just the *New York Times, Philadelphia Inquirer/Daily News, Wall Street Journal, Los Angeles Times, Chicago Tribune,* and *Washington Post,* the biggies that have gone online. Even small papers, such as the 113-year-old weekly *Minnedosa Tribune,* based just across the border in Canada from North Dakota, have Web sites some of which, like the *Tribune,* already are profitable.

Those attending the annual Interactive Newspapers 1998 conference were told of the great opportunities of cyberspace. They also were told that now the millions of dollars in newspaper display ad revenues that have migrated to direct-marketing companies can be diverted back to newspapers through this technology. "In fact," said Peter Cox, head of Cox Interactive Media, "Web technology provides an economical means for newspapers to gather the kinds of data needed to support their own targeted advertising programs that can compete with the direct marketers." For example, most news Web sites offer free access but require users to register. Thus they are able to amass a database of demographic data that can be used to target visitors for ads, according to criteria such as age, income, gender, and hobbies. Even the *New York Times,* a relative newcomer to these virtual newspapers, requires users of the site to register and give key data.

Of the 1,520 daily newspapers, some 700 now have sites on the World Wide Web. And *Editor & Publisher* magazine found that "newspapers are loud and clear about keeping access to their Web sites either free or at a nominal cost. Right now, 89 percent do not charge for access to any portion of their online projects—and 85 percent say they do not plan to charge in the future."

Actually, as of this writing, among conventional large daily newspapers only the *Wall Street Journal* charges subscriptions for access to any part of its online daily. The *New York Times* charges overseas businesses $35 a month for access to its Web site but keeps the site free to registered readers in North America.

## Paying Subscribers Call for Freebies

*Slate*, the Microsoft-backed online magazine, decided to ask its audience to become paying subscribers. It initiated its pay-for-news policy in March 1998, so its "daily serving of features and comments on news, politics, and culture" was declared off limits to any Web surfer who doesn't shell out $19.95 for a yearly subscription. It does, however, still offer a free "front porch"—its home page.

An analyst for Forrester Research thinks *Slate* is making a mistake by taking the big hit in circulation (only 17,000 paid subscribers initially, providing only $340,000 annual revenue, while estimated annual operating costs are $45 million). These small circulation returns will reduce ad income. "As far as I'm concerned," said Forrester Research's reporter, "it's an advertising-driven business."

The same analyst, Bill Bass, told the *New York Times* that to change anything "you have to have a project that is very unique." The Times added that *Slate* "arguably has the depth and analysis of print, the immediacy of radio and television, the bells and whistles of Web sites . . . [it] calls itself a weekly yet updates its content daily." Perhaps proving Forrester's point is the folding of two Web sites, *Word* and *Charged*, during the same week as the introduction of *Slate*'s new policy, both of which had charged for access.

There's no question there are problems. Online newspapers are struggling to produce even a fraction of the revenues of comparable print advertising. One reason is that audience measurement techniques are questioned by advertisers. Another thing that doesn't please advertisers is that uniformity of rates and sizes of online display or banner ads is nonexistent.

Despite the problems, Jupiter Communications forecasts that total spending for online advertising will vault from $300 million in 1996 to $5 *billion* by 2000.

Who is creating and selling the majority of newspaper online ads? Would you believe it's "the [advertising] agencies, because the newspaper people just weren't up to speed," says Knight-Ridder's national online ad manager Jean Edwards.

So how many staffers do such online publications require? The survey showed that typical full-time staffing is one advertising employee, one technical employee, and two editorial employees. That's likely to change; a strong need for cyber-ad–savvy people for online newspapers is just around the corner.

## AGENCIES MUST LEARN NEW-TECH ADVERTISING

Late in 1997, chairman Niall FitzGerald of Unilever Corporation, which makes Ragu products, warned that ad agencies need to expand their media services. Ragu has had its own Web site for two years, he says, and has registered more than 1 million hits.

He stressed the fact that "new technology [requires] new copywriting skills and the ability to understand not just the brand but the nature of the medium and the likely state of mind of each consumer participant." He called his warning a challenge to agencies that they need to look beyond TV. "I do not want to have to choose between an agency that understands interactive advertising and one that understands how to turn shopfronts into giant billboards," he said. "I want them to be good at both."

Substitute the words "job seeker" for "agency" in FitzGerald's remarks, and his advice is also advice and a challenge to you.

His predictions, which appeared in October 1997 *Advertising Age*, were that "TV/Internet/wireless shopping will skyrocket. The consumer marketplace is undergoing an unprecedented redefinition, making it much more difficult to chart a true course toward the millennium."

### Upstart Specialist Agencies

The story—again from *Advertising Age*—goes like this.

> In late 1995, a start-up online media buying and planning company called i-Traffic [with mega clients such as Walt Disney Co. and BellSouth] opened its doors.
>
> Media executives at traditional ad agencies widened their eyes in curiosity. But figuring their

shops could do the same work that an upstart could, these agencies continued to sign clients that wanted World Wide Web design and advertising.

Now, millions of dollars in online ad spending later, agencies are increasingly realizing that online media billings are growing faster at independent upstarts than at traditional media departments.

It's not surprising that large agencies are struggling to create their own interactive media-buying divisions. However, there's a belief among many clients that interactive media business should be handled by separate units. In other words, the thinking is that the agencies should go with the specialists. Smaller agencies are going with them because online media campaigns need many work hours, even on small budgets.

The attempt, or threat, to separate conventional agency functions does not, however, lessen the escalating need by agencies and corporate in-house advertising departments for people who understand how cyber advertising works. Agencies and advertising departments need to establish for their clients what works and what's best for all concerned.

Perhaps you should keep specialty agencies, such as i-Traffic, in mind when you line up potential employers if you have the knowledge, training, and desire to tie up with a cyber-ad company.

## GREAT NEED FOR NET SAVVY

Whoever spoke the following words may have made the understatement of the year: "The need for people who understand Net advertising is great indeed."

The need for multimedia-degreed employees is high enough that it's paying off in hard-cash returns for the Net-savvy. *Advertising Age* reports that many agencies are "putting such a premium on these kinds of degrees that they're offering entry-level salaries at twice the level of graduates without some multimedia education." Actually, this kind of advertising background can mean the difference in entry-level salaries of $25,000 to $30,000 in other areas, to $40,000 to $45,000 to do Net work.

If you're not interested in becoming an advertising cyber-brain, here are some analogies that may help convince you it's important to at least become new-tech literate so you'll still be around a few years ahead. Keep in mind that Royal and Underwood typewriters aren't here anymore because they refused to admit that electricity was coming to typewriters. And Singer no longer makes sewing machines.

Further in the chapter we'll give you some tips for locating online-savvy jobs.

## WHAT HAPPENS WHEN ADVERTISING BECOMES INTERACTIVE?

Advertising icon Tom Cuniff says IA advertising may be the most powerful selling medium ever, because "instead of endlessly pushing people to buy, we're able to do what the smartest salespeople do: Let the prospects sell themselves. And we're able to measure precisely how well it works: The longer people choose to interact with the ad, the more likely they are to buy."

Another advertising guru, Andrew Batkin, says that the best way to visualize interactive advertising is to picture the ideal way to get consumers involved in the advertising message. And IA does just that.

Pretty strong reasons for advertisers to jump aboard!

The blurring of the editorial zone and the advertising zone has been a problem for IA advertising from its beginning, but as one professional noted, "That's an issue you face in every medium."

The all-out major issue is that this new advertising form overcomes traditional methods where customers are passive and bombarded with messages. In this new form, they must do the seeking to find the advertisers. Savvy users of IA advertising know to provide "value-added" content to their messages.

### A Site to See—Net-Literate Advertising

Online, on paper, or aboard any other ad vehicle, it's essential to success that the people writing the message know how to do it.

The information in a February 1997 ad for *DoubleClick Network* can serve as a beginner's tipsheet to learn the essentials for "creating effective online campaigns." First, the copy asks, are you aware of the Internet's marketing potential? Marketers were faced with a similar question about TV fifty years ago. They realized the potential and used moving pictures to inform and influence their audiences. The Web has introduced a new set of communication tools.

Then the ad copy lists "four factors that influence the success of an online campaign."

**Targeting.** A brilliant ad that's not seen by the right audience is useless. On the Web, you can target individuals. There is no waste. Target marketing has never been so precise and so cost-effective.

**Creative.** Developing effective ad banners on the Web is a challenge for even the best creatives. (TestIt!, a DoubleClick product, is named as a service that evaluates banner creative before executing a complete advertising schedule.) Within 48 hours, the ad states, you can see which ads achieve the highest response.

**Frequency and banner burnout.** How many times should someone see your ad? Too few and your message doesn't have an impact. Too many and you're wasting money. After the fourth impression, ad banners burn out and average response rates drop under 1 percent. To ensure strong response, you should control frequency and rotate banners in a series.

**Content.** Placing an ad on a site that has relevant content will almost always result in higher click-through and more effective branding. Select the Web pages, sites, or editorial your banners appear within. (Another DoubleClick product, Editorial Targeting, is also plugged.) It assists media planners by transparently

scanning millions of Web pages. Ad banners are
dynamically delivered to pages that match your criteria.

Even though the DoubleClick copy is an obvious sales message for
its own products, it includes excellent advice.

## Ready, Aim, Hit the Target

The big question for advertisers always is who's listening, who's
watching, who's reading our ads? For Net advertisers, however, the
key question should be not just who are these people, but who are
the browsers and who are the buyers. Who they are dictates
message content and the way the message is constructed.

A new demographic ad service was introduced late in 1997 that
allows precision ad targeting. The process, by America Online, can
reveal more than 200 kinds of information about individuals, which
furnishes some pretty great pictures of consumers. Ameritech and
Tropicana Dole Beverages, among others, signed on to use the
targeting service. An executive of MetroMail's Internet Services
Group told *Advertising Age* that "the objective is to serve ads aimed
at people's interests and engender better results." Apparently it's
working because there is evidence that consumers are ready for ad
targeting and that they appreciate it.

This is just one example of how online advertising is living up
to the promise of the Web—using the medium's unique
interactivity to build one-to-one relationships between brands and
consumers.

## Pinpoint and Capture that Consumer

Capturing Internet advertising dollars, however, is a whole other
contest. Games that provide substantial incentives to prospective
players is what Michael Paolucci and John Waller, whose Web site
is called Riddler, came up with.

In order to play, reports *Forbes* magazine, you have to provide
some juicy personal data: age, e-mail address, occupation, favorite
trade magazines and television shows. Further, players must

promise not to reveal the information they give Riddler to outside firms. Riddler "uses the information to steer each ad to the right eyeballs." When advertisers place an advertisement on Riddler, they know it will be seen by every surfer who comes through, because you can't play unless you click on the ad. Advertisers are charged 25 cents a hit by Riddler.

Riddler's method has attracted the biggest advertisers, such as Royal Caribbean Cruise Lines, Toyota, and Snapple. There's little wonder that Web surfers are more likely to visit Riddler's site where they click on a logo and get a full-screen ad, when you compare it with the "other" method of Web advertising that merely throws corporate banners onto screens. The fact is that only 3 percent of people who see a banner actually click on it.

## Building Web Ads

Newspapers have two types of advertising: display and classifieds. The Net has basically four types: banners, click-through ads, sponsorships, and classifieds.

Before we go any further let's de-baffle the bafflegab, in alphabetical order.

- Banners are the tiny display ads you might call cyber billboards
- Classifieds are as we've known them since the 1700s, an effective, low-cost way to promote products, services, and job seekers to large numbers of people
- A click-through is when a user clicks on the ad to retrieve the ad and the advertiser is then charged on a per-user basis
- Sponsorships are offered on Web pages (Sponsorships are when a company sponsors an entire Web site as the only advertiser.)

Advertising on the Web is still in an experimental stage. There are no cut-and-dried rules and not many do's and don'ts. There are, however, indications of fundamental requirements each ad must embrace. We know there are three essentials: sound, action, and video. But the mold that the sound, the action, and the video take are as broad as all creativity.

There's another element that is essential to Internet advertising—it must be interactive. Unlike other advertising, online advertising consumers request information. It's not just advertisers dispensing a message and hoping the medium's audience will take the time to read it or view it or hear it and then react to their messages.

Both content and entertainment are known to be important. As are things that spur action, such as free samples.

Another highly important principle behind successful online advertising is a dedication to keep it fresh. There are any number of statistics that show that without changes, updates, new information, and a new look every two to three weeks, the message is passed over. That means that after two to three weeks, you might as well get off the site.

Of course, the message itself is all-important. Your first challenge is to use the message to establish trust. The problem originates with so much trash being posted on so-called news sites. Any individual or business can publish something that looks like a newspaper. As more and more "legitimate," traditional, high-quality newspapers go on line, perhaps they'll establish ethical news standards the public will recognize and demand. There's also garbage in a lot of online advertising; perhaps ethical advertising standards will also be improved by authentic newspapers establishing advertising ethics.

Beyond establishing trust, be sure your Web ad:

- Stresses benefits for the customer
- Speaks right out—don't be vague or misleading
- Spells out exactly what is included, how much it costs, and how it will be delivered
- Always asks for immediate action, such as by fax or by the automatic mail reply system called mailbot (Mailbot is a software program that automatically processes e-mail for Net users.)

Foolproof advertising hasn't been invented yet. Only testing gives indications of what works with which group and where it works; so ongoing reviews are required.

## Tech it Easy—Locating Graphics on the Web

If you plan on joining an agency, an in-house ad department, or a resource group—or you're merely looking for art to use in your presentation—here's information that may help. Perhaps the most helpful in finding the art you're looking for is the Clipart Directory. It lists different pages, ranging from general clip-art collections to sites for very-specific needs.

Joe De Rouen in *Current Technology* magazine calls ArtToday "the granddaddy of all clip art sites." There you can find hundreds of thousands of images, categorized into several easy-to-search areas, such as clip art, photos, and animation. And within each category are several more categories. "You can, for instance, view thumbnail images of the photos you're interested in, then either download them or add them to a download cart to be transferred later." ArtToday isn't free. The site costs $17.95 a year to access, but "with that you get all of the photos, animation, and clip art you can download," says DeRouen.

## HOW DID IT ALL START?

Early in the 1990s interactive media were being called "the great zero-billion-dollar industry." It was Barry Diller who almost single-handedly started the interactive TV craze in 1993 by buying QVC, a little-known home shopping channel that took it all into cyberspace!

Today the thriving interactive industry is really *active*. It includes home shopping and infomercials, education services, travel assistance, CD-ROMs, interactive 800 numbers, video malls, and commercial online services.

As one executive describes interactive, "We've always talked back to our television sets. Now, the TV sets [and our computers are] listening." IA media permits one-on-one communication, viewer to advertiser, and lets online consumers quickly locate the lowest price for a product or service. It's also where consumers are able to search interactively for electronic ads on demand.

Ford cars and the J. Walter Thompson advertising agency were one of the first to go for interactive advertising. In one commercial, Prodigy Online users were invited to explore a Ford car by clicking on different parts of the car. If they clicked the mouse on the hood, for example, a model of the engine appeared. Clicking on the engine brought up a full description of its mechanics.

The Ford interactive ad succeeded in its purpose—to lead consumers from the initial arousal of interest to the point of sale.

## WHAT'S NEXT FOR ONLINE ADVERTISING?

Texans have said it for years, but now with Internet advertising it has much greater meaning. "The future ain't what it used to be!"

Who knows where the Net is headed or how great its success will be? Cartoonists Bunny Hoest and John Reiner believe its success is sufficient that heaven already lists its address over its entry gate as www.heaven.com.

Another ad for DoubleClick asks the question—and gives its own answer—What's Next for Online Advertising? The answer is a copywriting example that reads like the first page of a novel.

> You are deep in the heart of the forest, with only one shot left. Carefully you pull the arrow from your quiver and slide it into your trusty bow. Without hesitation you pull back and fire. Your arrow cuts through the air and sinks into the target.
>
> A scene from Sherwood Forest? An exciting new video game? Neither. Actually, it's an example of the latest advancement in online advertising: a Java-enhanced banner from First Virtual for United Cerebral Palsy Associations that allows users to test their archery skills and then make a donation—all within the space of a standard ad banner.

In a special supplement about creativity and business marketing in *Advertising Age*, Alan Brody spells out what he believes is ahead.

> If you put it all together, which is what the [ad] industry is desperately trying to do, the emerging future looks something like this: all new-media elements will be connected somehow. Ads will refer you to Web sites; CD-ROMs will house the graphics too complex to pass over the Web, and people will come to rely on the interactive media because it offers a richer style of entertainment—or at least an adjunct to linear styles of entertainment—while shopping and doing business.

Brody also states that the ability to offer the information people want is becoming so critical that Hotwired's slogan is: "We waste our time so you don't have to."

## MORE AHEAD THAN JUST THE WEB

They're here. Digital compositing—a technique to insert former TV and movie stars into current videos. And CCDs—charged coupled devices that are used in filming and new camera systems.

Of course, there's also e-mail—direct mail advertising without the postage stamp. And fax advertising. Videotex. CD-ROM. By the time you read this, who knows what else there will be.

They're here and they're today, and probably there are more coming tomorrow. Technologies that are rising across the horizon are mind-boggling—such as digital TV, DVDs (those long-promised digital video discs), and PDAs (personal digital assistants), thought by many to be the most significant innovations since color picture tubes in the 1950s.

### Going "Digital"

It's the digital age, and in 1994 *Style* magazine warned, "Have a valium, Madison Avenue." Today any visual can be digitized, stored, and made available at the touch of computer keys. Visuals and sound have been digitized, which reduces the cost of Internet and TV commercials. Digital cameras that can shoot in natural light *without film* will be a part of our everyday world.

PDAs have been around for several years, but initially they were priced way too high. With them users can send and receive faxes, make phone calls, and get e-mail messages—an ideal medium for e-mail and fax advertising messages. You might liken them to electronic Yellow Pages.

So established is digital TV that the FCC has set forth a plan that would make current analog stations go dark, leaving only digital channels, by the end of 2006.

The Newspaper Association of America is so concerned about the impact of digital electronics that they established a group called Task Force on Digital Advertising "to resolve issues relative to the processing of digital ads."

Digital ad *delivery* is here, too. After nearly a decade of receiving display ads electronically, the newspaper industry now offers digital delivery. For advertisers it eliminates the costs of outputting the same ad dozens of times and delivering the materials by courier to each paper.

An ad for Sony D-2 digital delivery says, "A digital copy isn't just a dub. It's a clone. An exact replication of your original commercial. Digital makes sure the high quality of your production comes through generation after generation . . . [with] the same true color, sharp resolution and crisp, clear sound as your original."

It's so popular that even Office Depot has signed Associated Press's digital ad delivery service, AP Adsend, to transmit about 50,000 ads per year for its 512 stores across the country.

## Digital Wireless

*Current Technology*, the "Regional Magazine For Technology and Business Computing," explains the impact [DW] will have and the way it works in a wonderfully easy-to-understand fashion.

"It's 2000-something," says contributing writer Bridget Mintz Testa. "I have a phone number. And if you have that number, too, you can fax me, phone me, or e-mail me, all at some breathless bandwidth, no matter where in the world you or I may be. Even though [I may have] no landline connections, I'm wirelessly connected to the rest of the human universe. And I can take that connection with me, anywhere in the world." Can you imagine what this is going to mean for advertisers?

"Of course," says Testa, "before we get to 2000-something, the wireless industry is going to change a bit. That's happening right now, as analog and digital services fight it out for customer share." "Obviously," she says, "digital is going to win (because the moral of the 20th century is that digital is delightful—and better than analog)."

Wireless technology is headed for a great future mainly because, Testa believes, one of today's major trends is a greater roaming capability both at home and abroad. "Wireless communication is the key in the worldwide information revolution. In terms of data, it's just starting."

Are you ready—and prepared—for this digital age in advertising? Too bad too many advertising agencies aren't—yet! But they're smart enough to keep searching for the people who are.

## E-mail Over "Snail" Mail

This is an advertising medium that's not likely to go away soon. It's available anywhere there's access to a computer and modem. It's so simple that anyone who knows how to type can use it. It's fast and has the same reach and the same immediacy as the telephone and digital. And it's cheap—users don't have to worry about postage or a delivery time lag as they do with postal mail.

This kind of traffic is very ad friendly. However, complaints about junk e-mail—especially the automated bulk mailings known on the Net as "spam"—are increasing. Pending lawsuits about the problem indicate changes and regulations are ahead.

There's another difficulty for product advertisers that Hank Ketcham gives voice to through "Dennis the Menace." Dennis's mom is sitting at her computer as Dennis tells a friend, "The trouble with e-mail is that you never get any packages." The problem of delivery of e-mail ad orders undoubtedly will be solved in the very near future by some as-yet-unknown new technology.

In the meantime, and in the future, attracting viewers and getting them to return to the site and place orders takes the skill of an ad pro. Not your regular, out-of-the-past, conventional ad pro, because as Media Lab's Nicholas Negroponte has said, "The Web is not a market, it is a culture." And that culture wants its free information in a form they connect with—news, games, education, graphics, services. Here, viewers can talk back, and if they don't "connect" with the advertiser, they're gone.

The point of all this is that no business, and especially no advertising business, can ignore the changes that are here and now, and yet to come. It's past being obvious that the people who seek jobs in just about any industry—but particularly the advertising business—must have this kind of knowledge and training.

## FINDING NEW-TECH, ONLINE-SAVVY JOBS

So, how do you go about finding these jobs? Easy—go where the recruiters are searching, and that's in the trade press, in newspaper sources, and in Net Classifieds for lower- and mid-level jobs. Search firms are more likely to be used in the hunt for executives, however.

An article in the *New York Times* in March 1998 by Susan J. Wells offered information about hunting jobs via the Web. It told readers that "With Internet access and a mouse, job seekers today can search vast collections of available positions worldwide and apply or post their credentials in seconds." Internet Business Network is one of a few companies that count and rank the seemingly endless array of job sites. It estimates that its 1998 index will identify some 20,000 career sites, the *Times* reported.

The Riley Guide, at www.dbm.com/jobguide, offers a good introduction to the wealth of job information available. The site also includes an overflow of information for beginner's on how to conduct a job search on line.

Internet Business Network, at www.interbiznet.com, annually ranks best sites by industry, ease of use, and comparative offerings. The *Times* article also listed seven other sites to visit:

- Online Career Center: www.occ.com
- Career Mosaic: www.careermosaic.com
- The Monster Board: www.monster.com
- Career Magazine: www.careermag.com
- Career City: www.careercity.com
- E-Span: www.espan.com
- Career.com: www.career.com

And finally, the *Times* suggested using an online search engine like Yahoo (www.yahoo.com/business/employment).

Huge numbers of jobs aren't being advertised, however. For those, you must do your own exploring. "Online recruiting has augmented but not replaced the more tried and true ways, like referrals, classified ads, job fairs, networking, and private recruiters," a spokesperson for the Society for Human Resource Management said.

Recruiters rely heavily on graduating university students, so they go "on-site" at universities and conduct intensive interviews there. Also, watch for job or career fairs. If a company is large enough to have its own human resources department, it's likely to seek out these fairs and participate with its own exhibits.

Most newspapers with a Web site include job ads. And single newspaper sites are a particularly good place for a company to post job ads to attract local residents, says an article in *Online*.

# chapter 12

## Getting Ahead in the Industry

Two of the three boxes in a Scott Adams "Dilbert" comic strip are about getting promoted. It has value for those actually looking to advance in the workplace, presented with humor as only Scott Adams's characters offer it.

The first box rightly advises, "If you want to be promoted, you have to be highly visible."

The second box says, "Ask questions at meetings. But make them easy so you don't embarrass your boss." More good advice.

And then the not-so-wonderful-advice in the third box: "If there's an accident in a company car, where should we bury the survivors?" The boss replies, "I usually put them in the trunk."

True, if you want to be promoted, you do have to be highly visible. And also true, any time you ask questions they should not embarrass anyone, particularly the boss. But there's a lot more to getting ahead in any industry—particularly in the advertising industry—than the above two "musts."

In addition, you should know the benefits of networking, the ways it can work for you, how to use it—and then plan to practice it the rest of your life. Also, use the canons for writing pay-attention-to-me-I-can-help-you letters as another must for lining up interviews that will move you ahead in the business. And of course it's necessary to know how to handle the most important part of the entire process—the interview.

This is the chapter that offers counsel about these essentials for getting ahead in advertising.

## SECRETS OF NETWORKING—THIS BUD'S FOR YOU!

Networking may be one of the most productive *lifelong* career management tools in your toolbox. We're not talking about the list of names you use to get an immediate job, then toss or file where you'll never find it again. This *networking list* is made up of people who become your business buddies. As career employment newspaper columnist Joyce Lain Kennedy describes it, "Real networking requires deep, ongoing, caring and sharing interactive practices for all phases of your life."

Networking isn't new, but you'd think it was by how few people seriously put it to work. Networking means lining up people who can help you in your job search, who can give you information and background facts about jobs, can tell you where the jobs you want are, and yes, perhaps even open a door or two for you. Networking buddies are also comrades for you to lean on who will give you much-needed, over-the-shoulder advice. They're your *contacts*.

### Contacts and Referrals

"Contacts" and "referrals" are impressive words. Doubtless it was contacts that got the president or CEO of each agency or company you approach their jobs. Whether you're a newbie or a move-along, you absolutely must have contacts, and they become your network. If you haven't already begun gathering them, it's time to begin what should become a lifelong avocation—collecting contacts who fit into your network.

Contacts are everywhere. Teachers, alums, friends, friends of friends, absolute strangers who are in a position to help, perhaps even relatives, or friends of relatives. They're the ones who can offer feedback on that brainstorm you came up with—or they can brainstorm with you. They can lend an ear, give advice, point out where the jobs are. They can give you the background information that will help you get an interview that leads to a job, and they can give you names to contact—perhaps even provide personal introductions.

Beyond people, there are organizations that may be a direct line to exactly the individuals you want to contact. There's probably no better place than a local advertising club where agency people, company ad people, and media people gather for their own purposes and maybe to fulfill some of your purposes, too. They, too, may be looking for jobs—and one or two may be looking for someone to fill a job.

Test the waters by asking if you may attend a meeting *before* you commit to joining a group. If the group appears to be made up of members who can become the contacts you need, then join. Your initial purpose in joining is to mix and talk with members so you can get to know the ones you want to know and so they can get to know you.

Referrals are a part of the networking process. They come from your contacts. Referrals come from the people who can open doors, whose names or titles are of sufficient stature to catch the attention and ultimately the respect of the person you're petitioning. A referral can set up the friendly, receptive atmosphere you hope for.

## Don't Be Hesitant to Ask

Probably the reason more people don't call on family, friends, and business acquaintances is that they're reluctant to ask favors or to ask them to spend precious time getting and relaying the needed information. That's a worry you can toss right now. Almost everyone enjoys lending a hand to help someone. Actually, most people enjoy "showing off" their knowledge and who they know. Just think back to times you've been asked for information or assistance or recommendations by someone looking for a job and how pleased you were to lend a hand.

Don't be reluctant to ask people you may not know at all, either. When you want inside information about an agency or a company, the best way to get it is from employees, preferably former employees who usually will speak more freely than someone still on the payroll.

Agency or company executives you've never met can be another source of information. There's a general feeling that top-level people are inaccessible. Sometimes that's true, but not always. These people are often more approachable than mid-level people because they're on the lookout for new talent to fill their agency's or company's needs.

Keep abreast of when agencies win new accounts—that's nearly always when the agency needs new people—then call and ask to speak to the executive who heads up the service area you're interested in: creative, media, traffic, whatever.

## Part of Networking Is Asking Questions

Too many people foul up in their networking efforts by spending their time with contacts endlessly talking about themselves. They go to an organization meeting to make contacts and get information—and spend their time talking about themselves. Is there anyone more boring than the person who talks endlessly about himself and his accomplishments?

Asking questions, and then *listening*, is a far better way to *get* information. There's a complete section later in this chapter about questions—how to design them, how to ask them, and how to answer them. You may find Harvey Mackay's *Dig Your Well Before You're Thirsty: The Only Networking Book You'll Ever Need* (Doubleday, 1997) a big help in your networking efforts. (Mackay is also the author of an earlier bestseller, *Swim With the Sharks Without Being Eaten Alive*, Ballantine Books, 1996.)

## Say "Thank You"

People are happy to help when they're sure their help is needed and *appreciated*. Whenever someone, no matter how high up or how far down on your contact "scale," does something that helps you, write a thank-you letter. A thank you over the phone is *not* enough.

The same is true for the businesspeople you reach. Thank-yous are just good business manners. But you're cheating *yourself* if you say it rather than write it. True, a letter does exactly the same thing for recipients that spoken words do. The difference is that when those words come a few days later in the form of a letter, the person will think about you, remember you. And just maybe the letter may jog them into taking some other action on your behalf.

The Gale Research *Advertising Career Directory* makes some excellent points about the importance of writing thank-you letters. "A well-executed, timely thank-you note tells more about your personality than anything else you may have sent, and it also demonstrates excellent follow-through skills." Perhaps most important, "Thank-you letters may well become the beginning of an all-important dialogue that leads directly to a job."

Hopefully you're now convinced to put as much thought and time into these letters as any you write in your job search.

And speaking of letters—let's walk you through the techniques and give you some tips for writing letters that leave good impressions and accomplish what they're meant to.

## LETTERS . . . YOUR CORRESPONDENCE (OF) COURSE

There's nothing more personal than a letter, except the human voice. There are all kinds of letters to write in this job of getting a job. Networking letters. Resume letters. Cover letters. To answer an ad. To inquire about an opening. To get an interview. Thank-you letters. And sales letters. Yes, *sales* letters! But the fundamentals for writing any of them are basically the same.

Actually, you can put together draft letters and then adapt them as needed, according to each occasion and each person. A suggestion: As you write a letter for a specific purpose, set up a folder for that type of letter—cover, interview, networking/contact— and file it as the model for each time you write the same kind of letter.

### Job-Seeking Letter

Every job-seeking letter you write is a sales letter. Or it had better be. No matter how subtle, you're still pitching a product: you. So let's look at what makes up a dynamic sales letter.

First, mentally walk around to the other side of that desk and put yourself in the chair of the person to whom you're writing. Consider only what the *recipient* wants to know, because that's what you must write. He or she hasn't time to be interested in your interests, wants, or needs.

Second, be friendly when you say "hello." Friendly doesn't mean using fancy words, which will make you appear more pretentious than intelligent. It means write the way you speak.

Your letter's salutation—or "act of greeting" as *Webster's New World Dictionary* calls it—sets the reception mood. Each letter should address a specific person not a title. *Never* use "To Whom It May Concern."

A half-page ad for Formica in *Editor & Publisher* magazine tells it like it is. Three lines of enlarged typewriter type stand out in a considerable amount of white space.

```
Dear So and So,
This is how it feels when
people use your name generically.
```

The tiny logo line at the bottom of the ad says,

Remember. Formica is a trademarked brand, not a generic name for countertops.

It's important to always remember that people aren't generic either.

Third, just as with a news story, the lead paragraph must catch the attention of the reader and allude to what the story is about. As author Bradley Morgan in *Advertising Career Directory* (Gale Research, 1993) says, "If the opening sentence is dynamic, you are already 50 percent of the way to your end objective—having your entire letter read." Then he cautions, "Don't slide into it . . . your first sentence *must* make mention of what led you to write." After the lead paragraph comes the body of the letter with its pitch. And then the close, which *concisely* tallies the most important points and asks the customer to take advantage of the offer.

Fourth, make it simple. Write in a conversational style, as if you are *talking* to the person. Keep in mind that your letters are you. If your words are pompous, braggy, careless, stilted, or indifferent, that's how readers will picture you. You want readers to get to know the *real* you.

Keep sentences and paragraphs short to give readers' eyes a break, and keep the entire letter as short as possible. If it's involved, hard to understand, and lengthy you can count on the reader tossing it without bothering to plow through it.

Fifth, grab and hold the reader's interest by building a flow of information that carries the reader from paragraph to paragraph, from beginning to end. And be sure to write in the active, not passive, voice.

Sixth, tell them what's in it for *them*, how they—or the company or department for which they're responsible—will benefit. This is the basis of every great sales message—not selling, but offering benefits—benefits you *know* the potential buyer needs and wants.

Seventh, don't leave the *tact* out of *contact*. People are sensitive to words, so be very sure your words are polite and tactful. When we speak person-to-person, we have body language, facial expressions, perhaps a smile to help us tell what we mean. But in writing there are only the words, cold words on paper or possibly on an Internet screen. When you've checked and rechecked the words you've written, ask a friend who can be objective and truthful to read and react to your message and the way you've said it.

Finally, ask the receiver to take action—and indicate how.

These then are the basics of a good sales letter. Now let's look at specifics.

## More About Sales Letters

A book entitled *Sales Promotion Handbook* (Dartnell Corp., 1994) says exactly what we're saying today: "Every letter that goes out on the company's [your] letterhead should be a sales letter. Either it should sell goods [you] or it should sell good will."

When you substitute the word "your" for "company's" and "you" for "goods" it speaks directly and positively to what you must remember every minute that you write networking letters, resume letters, cover letters, letters to answer ads, letters to inquire about an opening or to get an interview, and thank-you letters. The same is true for *any* kind of letter having to do with your bid to break into or move around or up in the advertising business.

Think of the time you've already spent to build your network and to research where and to whom you plan to write letters for any of the reasons listed above. All that work can be undone by inept, awkward letters. On the other hand, it would be hard to estimate the numbers of people who now are doing exactly the work they love because of the degree of the appeal of the friendly *sales* letters they wrote while job hunting.

As the *Handbook* states, "Public relations people are well aware that the most important factor in giving character to a business is friendly letters." Friendly *words* are also the business of advertising. Here you have an opportunity to demonstrate your ability to use them.

Friendly letters are a key to sales, too, and again we say, your letters are *sales* letters. That's a major part in the art of getting your letters read.

## Getting Your Letters Read

- **Be brief.** Research proves that shorter letters are better. One way to accomplish this is to follow a couple of tips: Never use a long word when a shorter one will do. Lengthy sentences are a waste of words.
- **Use correct English.** Your letter speaks for your knowledge of English. Advertising, after all, is copy in one form or another, and ad copy must be in proper English, no matter how conversational or informal it is. No advertising employer is going to consider someone who doesn't seem to know and use good English.
- **Use plain English.** Keep in mind that fancy, pretentious words in a letter provide a picture of a stiff, ostentatious,

wordy person. Use of too much slang or hackneyed expressions may give a negative impression, too. And tone down those superlatives.

- **Come to the point quickly.** Picture the pile of mail that needs to be read by the busy businessperson whose attention you want to attract and influence. Say what you have to say in a cordial, friendly way—and don't waste valuable time.

- **Appeal to the addressee's self-interest.** "I" does *not* come before "you" in this correspondence. Deny the temptation to talk about yourself. Mentally sit in the chair of the person you're writing to and cater to that person's interests and needs, not yours.

The best way to "tell about you" without making the letter boring for the reader is to attach a brief bio (key word here is "brief"). If your letter sparks interest, the reader can flip the page and scan the bio.

In the bio, lead off with the information that is *most important to the recipient.* Tip: Leave details out. In other words, do what advertisers often do: tease a little. Make the reader want the details—and that means the reader will have to meet you in person in an interview or at least request more information by letter or with a phone call. Include a line that says something such as, "I know you're exceptionally busy, so I've kept this information to a minimum. If you wish details, just let me know."

## Rope 'Em in with Your First Paragraph

Think of your first paragraph as the lead in a newspaper story—or even a little like the headline in an ad. It must grab attention and interest. It must inform. And it should be no longer than a few lines.

Short paragraphs at the beginning of a letter tend to nudge the reader to read on. After three or four short paragraphs, the reader is either hooked or has stopped reading and tossed the letter. Once the reader is hooked, subsequent paragraphs can become a little longer because they detail the benefits the reader wants to know about.

Benefits! That's the key to the entire process. What do you have to offer this particular agency or corporate advertising department? This is the information that must come through loud and clear.

## Are "Hard Copy" Letters Dead?

Some people say that e-mail has kicked aside letters-by-mail. It certainly seems as if words on paper might be the dinosaur of modern business communication.

E-mail does have a plus. It allows computer users to send messages almost instantaneously on a network that is worldwide.

However, one of the major problems—stated in the language of the times—is that e-mail is "less worked-out." No one seems to care about punctuation, it tends to be shorter, and it also seems to be less thoughtful but friendlier. One e-mail writer describes e-mail correspondence as very staccato and with a tendency to misspell.

If you're asked to communicate by electronic mail, don't— repeat, don't—be tempted to throw the rules of correspondence aside. Be friendly. But also maintain the rules of good letter-writing. The e-mail, just as with hard copy correspondence, is all the receiver has to judge you by. It, too, is you.

## NOW FOR THE INTERVIEW

What follows may seem a little on the heavy side—heavy in terms of the amount of information offered. Once you get in the door, you won't stay long, if you don't make points. Here's a checklist to help you accomplish your goal.

- **Do your homework!** Before you ever go near a person for an interview, even before you initiate the appointment, *do your homework!*
- **Know as much about the person** who will be interviewing you—and of course about the agency or company he or she represents—as you can.

- **Line up the information you want** to obtain, the questions you want to ask, at the interview. Remember that questions should come from both sides of the desk and that they are a major part of an interview.

The secret to *asking* questions is knowing what questions to ask. So spend serious time lining up the questions you must ask to get the information you want. But be sure to also include one or two about the people you'll be talking to, to give them a chance to talk about themselves. Most people like that.

## Anticipate Their Questions

Be prepared for the general categories of interviewer questions. Although the questions you will ask are important, no questions are more important than those you're asked. Some interviewers follow a formula devised by LaRue W. Gilleland, which is called the GOSS formula, a memory-jogging acronym that stands for the words *goal, obstacle, solution,* and *start*. The GOSS formula covers:

**Goal-revealing questions.** What are you trying to accomplish? What's the real purpose of your strategy?

**Obstacle-revealing questions.** What problems do you face? What stands in your way now?

**Solution-revealing questions.** How did you handle the problem? What plan do you have for resolving the problem?

**Start-revealing questions.** When did you begin looking? When do you want to start?

Bestselling author Ron Fry's *101 Great Answers to the Toughest Interview Questions* (Career Press, 1996) range from question number one, which he calls the killer question—So, tell me a little about yourself?—to question number 101—When can you start? Another book you might find helpful is *The 90-Minute Interview Prep Book* by Peggy Schmidt (Peterson's, 1996).

There are many other potentially devastating questions you must be prepared for. Here are a few from Fry's book:

Why are you thinking about leaving your current job?

After being with the same organization for so long, don't you think you might have a tough time getting accustomed to another?

You've changed jobs quite frequently. How do we know you'll stick around if we hire you?

What are the biggest failures you've had during your career?

Tell me about the best/worst boss you've ever had.

What is the biggest mistake you ever made in choosing a job? Why?

If you're so happy at your current firm, why are you looking for another job? Will they be surprised that you're leaving?

What types of people do you find it most difficult to get along with?

What do you want to be doing five years from now? What are your most important long-term goals?

How do you behave when you're having a problem with a co-worker?

Do you know much about our company?

The salary you're asking for is near the top of the range for the job. Why should we pay you this much?

*Advertising Career Directory* lists other questions and gives advice about answers. They include:

Why do you want to be in this field?

Why did you choose our company?

What jobs have you held and why did you leave them?

What are your career goals?

Remember, however, that an interview is not just a series of questions. It's a conversation. And the friendlier and better informed you are, the more you'll take away from the meeting.

### Practice, Practice, Practice

Get the tape recorder or video camera out and rehearse for the interview. Call on a friend to act as the interviewer, then together critique your "performance."

## Write an Interview-Request Letter

Here are two examples of an interview-request letter: the not-so-good and the good. The not-so-good one has only one spotlight—"I"—from the first word to the last sentence. The good one focuses on the recipient. Often it's easier to learn from mistakes, so let's start with the poor one (see Exhibit 12.1).

Now, let's look at a sample letter that aims at the interests, concerns, and needs of the agency instead of the interview applicant (see Exhibit 12.2).

## Interview Do's and a Few Don'ts

If you clinched the interview, congratulations! Now make sure the big event goes smoothly.

- Be straightforward and forthright, and don't be elusive.
- Be positive, show enthusiasm for the job, and allow your personality to show through.
- Dress neatly and appropriately, in a conservative, professional-looking outfit. It was a wise person who said, "You never get a second chance to make a first impression." First impressions are often decisive.
- Be prepared with a sales pitch that describes your most valuable assets for this specific agency or advertising department. Be sure it runs no longer than a few minutes and that it doesn't sound memorized.

December 10, 1999
1100 Fox Hill Lane
Plano, TX 75050

Mr. Jere Johnson, Vice President
TopTown Advertising
751 Downtown Avenue
Plano, TX 75088

Dear Mr. Johnson:

I read in this morning's newspaper that TopTown Advertising has been awarded the Sports City account. I hope to obtain an entry-level position with an advertising agency that specializes in sports because that's my first love.

I attended the University of Texas at Austin on a sports scholarship, and I believe I have the experience and background in sports to be a substantial contributor on such an account. I also believe that my understanding of sports types and their buying habits has properly prepared me for a position with your agency.

May I have a meeting with you to discuss my career strategy and get more information about this account? I'll call your secretary next week to set up an appointment.

I appreciate your attention to my request and look forward to meeting you.

Sincerely,


Joe Middle-Initial-I Franklin

**Exhibit 12.1**

December 10, 1999
1100 Fox Hill Lane
Plano, TX 75050

Mr. Jere Johnson, Vice President
TopTown Advertising
751 Downtown Avenue
Plano, TX 75088

Dear Mr. Johnson:

When the story in this morning's newspaper about TopTown's assignment of the Sports City advertising account almost jumped off the page, I could only imagine how pleased you and your staff must be.

Your agency's record and outstanding reputation for the handling of sports-type advertising is well known in the advertising business. You undoubtedly have top talent in this field. However, if you need an entry-level person, wouldn't it be an asset to add someone who has some ground-level experience in sports and understands your clients' thinking and attitudes?

A brief resume is enclosed. I sincerely hope you will have time so that I may outline for you my strengths that will work to your agency's benefit. I'll call your secretary for an appointment at your convenience. I look forward to meeting you and learning more about TopTown Advertising.

Cordially,


Robert Goodfellow

Enclosures: Resume, "Testimonials" on my behalf

**Exhibit 12.2**

- Be alert to telltale signals of a dysfunctional organization, a control-freak boss, or that the company or boss operates on an ethical standard that is different than yours.

## Two More Essentials

In her book *The Ad Game: A Complete Guide to Careers in Advertising, Marketing and Related Areas* (Barnes & Noble Books, 1984) advertising professional Judith Katz said that "The most important parts of the interview are the last two things you do."

> One . . . before you leave, ask the interviewer who's to take the next action: will [he or she] get in touch with you, or should you call him [or her]? And, if it's the latter, when?
>
> Two [this can't be said too often] . . . before the sun sets on the day of the interview, send a short thank-you note: "Dear So and So: Thank you for taking time out of your busy schedule to talk with me about the account job with your agency. I look forward to another meeting with you and your associates.

"That's all," says Katz. "You'll accomplish two things: you'll show you have good business manners, and you'll get your name in front of that person's eyes for a second time. It could make the difference between your getting the job [and] not."

## RESISTING A-REST: FOLLOW UP, FOLLOW THROUGH

Ann Landers is known for her good advice. This is some of her wisdom you definitely should listen to. "The Lord gave you two ends. One for sitting and one for thinking. Your success depends on which you use. Heads [and head-directed follow through], you win. Tails, you lose."

Salespeople know that often it takes many callbacks before a prospect becomes a buyer. Whether your prospect is a networking buddy or a potential boss, it's your responsibility—not theirs—to make the next move. The thank-you letter is the first, immediate move. Then, after a suitable amount of time, there should be another follow-through effort on your part—to spark remembrance and, hopefully, action.

## A "Wooed" Awakening

Find a pleasant way to spark—or respark—the person's interest in you and your skills and abilities. Send along some new information, for example. Or, if you read something about the agency or one of its people, a congratulatory note can reactivate your name. Or, if you've just accomplished something that will interest or benefit the individual or the company, let the person know. The best way to respark interest is to restate how your abilities, talents, and skills fit right in with the agency's or company's needs.

None of this is easy. It takes work. It takes creativity. It takes time and investigation. But if you can find real reasons to write the follow-through notes or letters or make a rare telephone call that actually offers information, the hard work will pay off. (Telephone calls aren't as good as notes or letters because there's no way you can know that the time you call is convenient for the person you're calling.)

A letter or a call keeps you "visible" and is an indication of your sincerity and your dedication to staying with a project until it's done. That's a quality bosses appreciate and look for.

## THE INTERNET INTERVIEW

You knew it had to be. In this fast-paced, technology-driven business world, you knew interviewers would somehow find a way to use the Internet to conduct interviews.

Actually, it's used only as a means of preliminary sorting. Big corporations use it as a time-saving way to sift through too many applicants to glean the few who qualify for face-to-face interviews.

These firms usually ask candidates first to send their resumes. Candidates whose resumes stir interest are directed to Internet interviews. The Net interview usually includes forty to fifty questions and perhaps a think-piece of some kind.

There's no intention among those using this preliminary screening method to replace personal interviews. But for those companies with limited time and too many applications, Net interviews will continue because of their time-saving value.

The bad news in all this is that unless a company uses well-designed Internet interviews, it may screen out good people. The good news is that for both interviewer and interviewee a lot of time is saved. Basic, but pertinent, questions are answered before the formal interview, leaving more time in the in-depth face-to-face meeting.

# section III

# Looking Beyond Your First Job

Breaking into advertising was the hard part. All that work! The research. Getting to know yourself, your talents, abilities, wants, and *needs*. Building a network of contacts. Learning the ad business from inside. It was the groundwork, but it's done. And all the effort can work for you in your next move and other moves in the future.

Perhaps this is the right time to make some decisions about your future and where you want to go. Perhaps it *is* time to make a move. The chapters in this section are here to help you make those decisions, to make the move you decide is the right one—up the ladder, to a different zone within advertising, or out of it altogether because you've discovered it's not where you want to be.

Whatever your decision, whatever the move you decide to make, do it with enthusiasm. And hang onto all that advance work you've done so it'll be there for another move, at another time.

# chapter 13

## Time to Move Up? To Move Around? Or Out?

"Veni, Vedi, Velcro!" Those are the words Jack L. Woods told *Reader's Digest* he saw on an office bulletin board near its training room. "I came, I saw, I stuck with it."

So you came, you saw—but do you want to stick with it? Now is the time to look long and hard into your heart, as well as into your head.

It's possible that almost from the beginning you knew this isn't where you want to be. But the biggest question in that case is why? Is it because you don't like doing whatever it is you do—research, traffic, creative, or whatever? Or is it that you don't like the people in this particular group, and you feel sure that if you moved elsewhere you'd be happier?

It's also possible that you're happy and enthusiastic about the work you do, and from the very beginning you knew this was exactly the branch of the business you wanted to be in, but now you feel it's time to move up the ladder.

The Associated Press reported a national poll by Louis Harris and Associates in 1997 that shows most workers expect to move to another job within five years, even when they're satisfied where they are. Harris also reported that overall, 54 percent are very satisfied in their jobs.

Here's a tip for when you know you plan to stay where you are but want to move up. Tell your boss. Also discuss your goals. It helps to hear what your supervisor has to say about whether you should and can begin training for a step up and whether he or she sees a future for you in this organization. Your boss may also have advice about whether your goals and the direction you believe you want to take are good for you. Another tip is to keep your conversations with the boss to yourself.

## BEFORE YOU MAKE ANY DECISIONS, REEVALUATE

Reevaluation is an ongoing process in the advertising business. This is the time to get out the mirror and take that all-important second look at yourself and where you want to go. Later in this chapter we'll look more closely at conducting a productive personal "account review." Among things you'll have to decide is should you stay? Or maybe the low-hanging fruit has already been plucked from this tree. If that's the case, do you go for the fruit on another tree? Or should "the product" be repositioned?

Advertising is a truly multifaceted business. There are agencies, in-house corporate advertising departments, and resource groups. And within the business itself there are a host of different areas, from the most artistic and creative to the most systematic, efficient, businesslike departments, requiring sales, managerial, or analytical abilities.

A few years back a well-known advertising person said that the advertising business is made up of ten different groups of professionals: writers, artists, dramatists or theatrical-type producers, salespeople, marketers and decision makers, psychologists, statisticians, media analysts, financial managers, as well as people managers and project managers. With all the downsizing that's been done in recent years, most agencies are no longer that broadly staffed. But needs remain, and where they don't have on-site staff, they reach outside to resource groups for the expertise.

Also, today some agencies are expanding beyond advertising to include services such as direct marketing, public relations and publicity, even online publicity and advertising.

Where are you happiest?

You can answer most of your questions with an "account review."

## It's a Bold-Faced Life!

In the advertising business, there's a new challenge every day. It's a business of invention—to invent new ways to create that opportunity or to solve that problem.

It's a business that requires more of a commitment than other businesses. One of Madison Avenue's best-known creative executives, Jerry Della Femina, gives advice you may want to copy and mount over your desk or your computer workstation. He says, "[Advertising is] such a business of enthusiasm that if you're not totally excited about it, you should leave it." You might substitute the word "passion" for "enthusiasm."

The question then, before you go one step further, is do you have sufficient commitment to make your climb up the mountain? Is this what you really want?

The Lauren Fox story indicates the creative lengths to which some people are willing to go. Though she didn't have advertising training and wasn't looking for employment in the advertising business, she used immense creativity and an advertising medium to get her message out about her job hunt. She used an outdoor board along a busy interstate highway in Albuquerque, New Mexico, to reach a very untargeted audience.

"I'm looking for work! Call me at [telephone number]" was the message on the black-and-white billboard. And to put more zing into her message, she spent much of her time pacing along the billboard's almost- 4-foot-wide ledge, about 15 feet off the ground. With her cell phone in hand, she received a variety of calls from people curious about the sign, from people who were looking for work themselves, and from people who just called to find out if it was a real person up there.

There's no report about the success Ms. Fox achieved, but there's no doubt that an advertising agency or corporate ad department would love to cash in on her creativeness—if she has adequate advertising credentials.

## TAP INTO YOUR CREATIVITY

The Lauren Fox feat might also remind you that in the advertising business you *should* tap into your creativity to boost your salability. It used to be said that you either have creativity or you don't. No more. Now there's proof that everyone has creativity, but you must draw upon it. This is not to say that everyone has the artistic ability of Rembrandt, but creativity *can be learned*.

David Campbell said it's a myth when people tell you "There are those who have it and those who don't." The title of Campbell's book is pretty good advice for anyone, everyone, wanting to stick around in the ad business: *Take the Road to Creativity and Get Off Your Dead End* (Center for Creative Leadership, 1985).

Some of the best advice around about sparking your creativity is given by Denis E. Waitley and Robert B. Tucker in their 1992 book, *Winning the Innovation Game* (Berkley Publishing Group). Waitley and Tucker say that working with your ideas requires that you take the ideas seriously. "Pay attention when an idea occurs to you. Get into the habit of writing down ideas, evaluating them, and implementing the good ones. Improving your ability to come up with ideas is something that happens through practice."

## Change Is the Only Thing That Offers New Opportunity

A big part of your decisions should be influenced by your answer to this question: Are you ready to accept that this bold-faced life is changing almost hourly? An article from London, reported in the *New York Times* in February of 1998, indicates the degree to which the old rules among ad agencies are being turned upside down. And change is spreading like wildfire both here and abroad.

There's this "feisty young agency called St. Luke's, the wayward child of Chiat/Day," reports the *Times*, that is challenging some precepts of the advertising business and bucking the industry-wide trend toward consolidation. Just as Ms. Fox, "the billboard lady," did, this 100-or-so employee agency has come up with some of the most rule-breaking campaigns on either side of the Atlantic. The payoff—$35 million in new business, and counting.

Turning things upside down began inside the agency when its two leaders, Andy Law and David Abraham, decided to create an "intellectual experiment. The principle was you couldn't own people, but you could let people own the company," Abraham explains. The result, according to the *Times*, is a culture that seeks to stir the creative juices by making every employee an owner, with no corporate ladder to climb or glass ceiling to break through.

Another broken rule is their creation of specific brand rooms, designed to give the feeling of each client, and to encourage creativity among employees . . . uh, owners. For example, for a shoe account, the "brand room" is complete with footwear displays. And in the Eurostar brand room there are actual seats from the train.

"Working at St. Luke's is the difference between going to grade school and going to university," says Law. "At school the bell goes 'ding' and tells you what to do. We have no bell. Like a university, as long as you can create great stuff, we don't care how you do it."

Are you ready for a university with no bells telling you what to do? And for these kinds and degrees of change? They're here!

## If You Think You Made a Mistake, There's Plenty of Advice!

If you've discovered you love the advertising business but not the area you're in, you probably believe you made a mistake! If that's your belief, take to heart the old Portuguese proverb, "Stumbling is not falling."

It's not failing, either. Texans like to say, "It doesn't matter how much milk you spill, just so long as you don't lose the cow!" And keep in mind that Babe Ruth once held a season record for the most strikeouts.

So maybe you chose the wrong specialty, or you feel it's time for a change. Well, coping with change can be difficult, but what you heretofore considered to be a mistake can add up to a plus. You can make it work for you.

## Job-Jumping Can Be a Plus

Advertising is known perhaps as the "most moving" business around! It's fast-moving and fast-changing, with professionals moving from one agency to another, to the client side, even back to the place they moved on from. There's no discredit or dishonor. It's just the way the business is.

It's time for answers to a big question, though. How long should you stay in one place? The better question probably is how long should you stay in one *job?* Advertising and publishing guru S. William Pattis warns that if you were hired right out of college as a trainee, don't expect advancement immediately, not for a year or two. "From that point on," he says, "your progress can be rapid, if you are capable and if there are not a number of equally competent people ahead of you."

Pattis also advises that the rate at which you progress in advertising depends on your performance, ability to acquire the necessary skills, maturity, grasp of the business, and the success of your employer, whether it is an advertising agency, a studio, a small company or a corporate self-advertiser.

Another bit of advice. Job-jumping can give you broader experience and skills. But too much job-jumping can make you look unreliable.

## IT'S TIME FOR AN "ACCOUNT REVIEW"

Before you make any big job changes, take that all-important second look at yourself. But even before you do that, take a second look at the agency itself and how it operates. Do their people break through and climb the ladder, and how do they do it? Who are the people who make it? Does the agency draw mostly on outsiders, or do they promote from within? These answers give you a perspective on your chances regardless of the excellence of your personal "account review."

Reevaluation is an ongoing process among advertisers and their representatives. When it's done for a client in the ad business, it's called an account review. Accounts are periodically reexamined and assessed to assure both client and agency that previously set goals are being achieved or reset and that the accomplishments are what was expected. It's the same—or should be—for the people who work in advertising.

It's time to reevaluate the product—who are you? Go back to Chapter 5 for cues. Check whether you've created a strong "brand identity." Take a reading of your passion level—that absolutely, positively, essential ingredient that can't be taught. Ask yourself, should the product be repositioned?

Someone once said that the first time you did this it was just reading the recipe book. Now, it's sitting down at the table and really discovering the taste cravings you have.

Now is the time to reexamine your goals, the ones you set for yourself in Chapter 5. Then ask yourself, are you any closer to achieving your goals? (If you skipped the goal-setting process, stop now and do it. It is an essential part in answering your questions and getting you where you want to go.) As author Joe Griffith says, "The quickest way to get what you want is to identify what you want." Makes sense, right?

It can't be said too often, and if you've been in advertising for any length of time you've undoubtedly learned, that this business requires more of a commitment than most other occupations. As the founder and head of RJC International, Ray Champney, says, "You're not just performing a job, you are performing a service. It's an ongoing investigative process, and the most effective ways to reach your various target groups is not a rote-type procedure."

You've also had a chance to try it out and get a feel for whether or not you fit in the area you landed in. How does your personality and temperament fit where you are—and how will the fit be where you'd like to head? By now you should be able to assess your reactions and why others' attitudes and actions tend to press your button.

By now you've also had opportunities to peek over the transom at other areas and get a feel for what they're like.

## Seven Questions to Ask During Your Personal Account Review

1. Are you having any fun? That question tops the list because, as David Ogilvy, founder of Ogilvy & Mather, cautioned, "When people aren't having any fun, they seldom produce good advertising."

2. Are you really motivated? No matter how much the boss or people around you want you to succeed, they can't push you up the ladder unless you're willing to do the climbing yourself.

3. How's your passion level and what is your motivation? Is it a desire for wealth or a fear of being fired? Passion is a much better kind of motivation, because it lasts longer.

4. What's your priority? Setting priorities makes things happen. However, Hollywood legend Sam Goldwyn had a slightly different perspective on priorities. He said, "For as long as I can remember, whatever I was doing at the time was the most important thing in the world for me." That's the way successful advertising people feel, too.

5. Do you have a purpose? "The world makes way for a [person] who knows where [he or she] is going." Ralph Waldo Emerson said it back in his century—and it's just as true for the new millennium.

   Decide for yourself what your purpose is, and you'll learn as Alice did when she asked the Cheshire Cat, "Would you tell me, please, which way I ought to go from here?" The cat replied, "That depends on where you want to get to."

6. What's your value system? A set of personal values makes it easier to make decisions. And they keep you from losing sight of why you're in this business.

7. How strong is your will to win? Someone, perhaps Coach Vince Lombardi, said, "Winning is a habit. Unfortunately, so is losing." We know he did say, "Winning isn't everything, but the will to win is everything." Both observations are excellent advice here.

## HAVE YOU CREATED A STRONG "BRAND IDENTITY?"

In the ad business, how consumers perceive a product, their thoughts and feelings about it, and the expectations they have for it is essential information. This is "brand identity." Without it, they don't buy the product. Advertising is a means to create and perpetually reinforce a product's brand identity and image.

Every person looking to move up or around in the field must also establish his or her own brand identity in order to induce the right thoughts, feelings, and expectations among potential "consumers."

It used to be that the yardstick for whether an agency was doing its job was if it produced advertising messages designed to convince people to buy the product whether they wanted it or not. That, of course, has changed, and there's recognition that targeting the *right group* and building a brand identity and image that the targeted group trusts is a much more productive way to go.

Do what advertising people today do—ask questions about yourself that match questions about a product.

- What am I selling? What do I have to offer?
- Do I know which sales points, features, and benefits about myself to highlight in "my advertising," in my messages, in my job presentation?
- Have I kept up-to-date? Professor Leonard Schlesinger of the Harvard Business School calls this business "an industry notorious for eating its young." So it's essential that I keep my skills and training up-to-date, not just to get ahead, but to stay aboard.
- Which group of people in the advertising business want what I have to offer—what's my target group? Better yet, what group *needs* what I'm offering?
- Should I be directing my messages elsewhere? Where? The answers should indicate that to establish your brand identity you must concentrate on your prospects' wants and needs, using only your wants and needs that fit theirs.

## When Someone Else Does Your Account Review

It's called a performance appraisal. And the good part is that it provides information for the people sitting on both sides of the desk. For management, it's the thermometer that indicates the kind of job you're doing.

For you, it can help you develop and improve your own performance. But beyond that, "It's the most important document in your personnel file. Your appraisal will follow you throughout your career," says authority Mike Duncan. He also points out that "your company may use it for decisions regarding promotions, job transfers, salary increases, disciplinary actions, training requirements, etc." This vital advice is set forth in his book written for African Americans, *Reach Your Goals In Spite of the Old Boy Network: A Guide For African American Employees* (Duncan & Duncan, 1990). It should be read by everyone.

First-timers usually wonder how much and what kind of preparation they should do. Unfortunately they often decide that none is needed because the responsibility is on the shoulders of the appraiser.

Parts of your "Account Review" should provide you with the bulk of the information you'll need for this review. If you follow Mike Duncan's excellent advice, you'll do it yourself at least four times a year. He suggests you ask for blank performance review forms and complete them on yourself. What better way to update your account review and be prepared for an "agency review?"

## WHY DO CONSUMERS BUY?

There really are only two reasons people buy. They want or they need. In the ad business when hiring new employees, need almost always takes precedence over want. It doesn't always work that way with products, however. People often cave in to desire.

The pitch that has the greatest appeal *combines* need and want. That's the real winner, both for selling a product and when pitching yourself as the product.

## TIME TO MOVE AROUND

You've decided this is the business for you, and you believe you're in the right division of the business. But you also think it's best to move elsewhere, to another agency.

How do you know when to make plans to leave the agency where you are now? There are several answers.

- When you recognize there's nowhere to go where you are
- When you realize there can be no increase in pay
- When you see that the organization is so big that you're literally lost in the crowd
- When the organization is so small there's little challenge or diversity among clients and in the work you do

A word of advice—give yourself time for whatever move is right. Give yourself an extra amount of time if the move is headed outside the agency. You'll need sufficient time just to look for possible openings—and then to check out the organizations that offer the openings and the people within them.

Now a word of warning—do not move when it means you must take a pay cut or when you must take the same or a lesser position elsewhere, no matter how desperately you want the change. Such changes go on your record, which future employers want to see and from which they'll undoubtedly make assumptions, such as that you had problems where you were, that you couldn't get along with the boss or other employees, and that you aren't the person this company wants and needs.

## There's Help to Navigate Job Changes

Thomas Edison's advice can help. He said, "Everything comes to him who hustles while he waits." But there's much more concrete help available and at a price that should please and get you through the difficult period of changing jobs or careers.

The assistance is from the Cuyahoga County Public Library in the Cleveland, Ohio, area. It's called ABLE—*the Adult Balanced Life Enhancement Inventory*, and it's designed to help you examine how energies are being spent across six different life dimensions—physical, emotional, intellectual, occupational, social, and meaning/purpose.

One of ABLE's three authors is career counselor and head of InfoPLACE, a public service of the library, Martin Elliot Jaffe. To obtain a copy of the ABLE inventory and a user's manual, send a check for $5 to:

Cuyahoga County Public Library—InfoPLACE
5225 Library Lane
Maple Heights, OH 44137

## IS IT TIME TO MOVE—*OUT*?

This may be the hardest decision of all.

As we said earlier, it's possible that almost from the beginning you knew this isn't where you want to be. You must answer some very big questions: Why do you think you want out? Why don't you like the work you're doing? Is it too structured, too repetitive—or not structured enough? Or is it that you don't like the people you work with—or the type of people who work in this zone?

There are people who literally hate the position they're in but stay in it for a lifetime. They are never successful. And they never realize the satisfaction of achievement or reach the level of pay they could if they'd been in a different field, one that fits their abilities and their personalities. Usually, financial need is the dictator that keeps them in such situations.

Only you can know whether you belong in the advertising business. But if you recognize and admit it isn't the right place for you, call on business and personal friends, your network of contacts, anyone, everyone who is in a position to give you a hand.

By now, surely you are aware, people are willing to help. Depending on the nature of the person who is your boss, you might even call on him or her for help. If you have a good relationship, he or she undoubtedly will want to help—for two reasons. To help you, but also to help the company. Finding someone to replace you who truly loves the work you're doing undoubtedly will benefit the company. So it will work both ways.

## Can't Decide What To Do? Toss a Coin!

That's advice from Sigmund Freud no less, and the person who received it reacted just as you probably do. "I can't believe it! You, a man of science, guided by senseless chance." Freud then made clear how the action can work for you. He said,

> I did not say you should follow blindly what the coin tells you. What I want you to do is to note what the coin indicates. Then look into your own reactions. Ask yourself: Am I pleased? Am I disappointed? That will help you to recognize how you really feel about the matter, deep down inside. With that as a basis, you'll then be ready to make up your own mind and come to the right decision.

That's it then. Are you ready to pack your climbing gear?

# chapter 14

## Pack Your Climbing Gear

Because this is advertising, and it's a highly introspective business, there's no cut-and-dried "Here's-how-you-do-it" formula for getting up the mountain.

Highly respected advertising professional Raymond J. Champney made the statement that it's essential for those in advertising to be introspective, too. That means it's time to look into your mind, your feelings, and do a little analyzing of yourself in relation to continuing to live in the world of advertising.

Champney, founder and owner of RJC International, compares this time in your life with what happens daily in the ad business. "It seems that every day you have to invent new ways to solve a problem or to create an opportunity. For some people this is the best life." There are others, Champney says, "who can't take it. They can't put up with the daily changes, with the pressures that sometimes go along with coming up with solutions and new programs. There are a lot of people like that."

One of my very good friends who worked with me at McCann Erikson went through these problems. He was a great guy, but he thought he didn't like the area he was in. He wanted desperately to get out of production and traffic and into account services. And he did just that, became an account executive for a beer account, and then found out he didn't like it. What he really liked after all, was doing traffic and production. So he gave up the account position and went back to being one of the best in the business—in traffic and production.

And there's nothing wrong with that. When my friend got into the business he made an effort to learn as much as he could in all the different categories. Then when he wanted to move into the new account position he was able to demonstrate an understanding, a willingness and a desire to do it that got him the change. But when he got there he found he didn't enjoy dealing with clients on a daily basis, and having to deal with the various agency departments. He found that all he wanted to do was go back to doing what he knew how to do best, what he was most comfortable and happy doing— which was production and traffic.

What all this says is, be sure you take your rappel gear—that "double rope" that can get you back where you really want to be.

## WATCH FOR CHALLENGES

Don't limit yourself, and learn to invent opportunities. This is a time to "uplearn," to become a master of change and tap into your resourcefulness and ingenuity as an opportunity spotter.

One of the wonderful things about the advertising business is that it's not what it used to be. Most agencies no longer are advertising-only agencies. For a number of years there has been a growing trend to offer services beyond traditional advertising— way beyond. These include direct marketing, sales promotion, and public relations and publicity. Now they're even including such areas as data analytics and Web site development. What this means, of course, is that your unplowed field of dreams has broadened to a grassland just waiting for you to stop by and do a little grazing. It also means you don't have to limit yourself. It means that you can continue to focus on the category/division/classification you're in—but you can, and perhaps should—continue to investigate and search out other areas of opportunity.

### Is It More Buck for Your Bang? Or Finding a New Opportunity?

Is it money you're looking for—or opportunity?

Don't stop with just an evaluation of your paycheck. With the escalating number of takeovers, with all the downsizing, demassing, shake outs, reorganizing, reinventing, and restructuring that agencies are going through these days, it's pretty safe to say that the bucks are where the opportunities are. Just as there's a stairway in job importance, there's a stairway in pay. Put aside pay for the moment, and think about locating opportunities and what that can mean.

For some people, opportunity-spotting is an instinctive process. If that's not a natural for you, "you can train yourself to see the patterns as you go about observing trends, patterns that can tip you to new opportunities," say Denis E. Waitley and Robert B. Tucker in their book, *Winning the Innovation Game*. They did a study and listed the five sources of innovative opportunities most often cited by the innovators in the study. Their book targets businesses, but the information is applicable here to your quest.

- Observe a trend and come up with a way of exploiting it
- Search for solutions to negative trends
- Look at your current activities, beliefs, and interests for ideas that might appeal to others
- When a present trend is running against you, come up with a new idea
- Watch what the competition is doing, and do it better

You'll need to read the book for the details and their explanations for making these five actions work for you. You probably can find a copy at your local library or through interlibrary loan.

Some of the best advice the authors give is in a series of questions to ask yourself what will help with the process of discovering "breakthrough ideas." They say the questions come from what they learned from innovators and suggest you use them to stimulate your thinking.

What can I offer that "they" aren't offering?

How can I position myself in a way that is different?

Where's the niche that hasn't been developed?

How can I *add value* to the service or product I now produce?

Where is the market inefficiency?

What would make this process or procedure more convenient?

What might my customer group want if it were available?

What do I really enjoy doing that I'd like to do more of?

How can I make a living from doing what to me is fun, challenging, and never boring?

What trends will change the assumptions my colleagues and competitors are presently making about my field?

Back to the question of salary. There are certain givens, such as that account service people are paid more than, say, those in traffic or production. There's good reason. Account service people are dealing with clients, keeping those clients happy—and happy clients stay with the agency, which generates income for the agency. Higher pay is also true for creative people. They are charged with putting together an outstanding product for the agency, so their services have tremendous value. They can be the highest paid within the agency, depending on their talent.

On the other hand, the earning capacity of people in line positions—traffic and production, for example—is based on seniority, degree of expertise, and on what that person's contribution to the agency can be.

## "If Opportunity Doesn't Knock, Build a Door"

Comedian Milton Berle said it, and he wasn't kidding.

An ad in *Brandweek* from Tusco Display offers words you could easily adapt to the message you want to deliver. We don't suggest you do so because as you'll see, it's a little too derisive for this purpose, but it gets an important point across. The headline reads:

*OPPORTUNITY is missed by most people because it is dressed in overalls and looks like work.*
*—Thomas Edison*

The body copy follows:

*If you're happy working with a P-O-P [Point of Purchase] company that tries to force the same old solution onto every new problem you bring them, then maybe you deserve the results you've been getting.*

*But if you want to work with a company that attacks every problem individually, then you definitely deserve the results you'll get from working with us.*

*Because here at Tusco, we know that for every problem there's a perfect solution—its own. And we won't stop working until we find it. That's a point of view you can peddle on your own behalf. It's what every advertising agency is seeking— people who won't stop working until they find solutions.*

## EVALUATE! MAYBE IT'S TIME TO TAKE A HIKE

- **In position.** It may call for negotiating yourself up the mountain
- **In pay.** Decide whether it's money you're looking for
- **Or opportunity**

In advertising, as with every business, there are line positions and management positions.

Are you hoping for some "swivel rights?" Do you have a deep-seated desire for a chair in management, at the head of the table?

You should know that most advertising jobs require a combination of abilities: creative, selling, investigative, and managerial. That doesn't mean everyone must have powerful talent in all areas, but it's been proven that people from just about any job zone can climb any of the job-zone ladders to reach a top management spot. That's the *only* way they get there. There are no entry-level management positions.

Management administers the business, and it requires knowledge about hiring and firing, about work assignments, meeting expenses, and showing a profit. In small- and mid-level agencies, managers usually continue to perform in their area of expertise—creative, media, sales, whatever.

If your goal is to become a chief executive, the rewards can be tremendous—hundreds of thousands of dollars a year, along with options and other perks. Remember that the air is thin up there, though. It's demanding, although physically and mentally probably no more so than in individual job zones that must produce exemplary results at a pace that meets client demand and production deadlines.

There are special demands on executives, for example, looking and acting the part, that aren't necessarily required in the departments they oversee. The rewards may be sweet in the executive suite, but it may be a difficult place to live for laid-back types.

There are also special trappings, clothing, especially, that go along with a key to the executive suite. Clothing is important in order to look the part. It's relatively easy for men: a suit and tie for dress-up occasions and coat off, rolled-up shirt sleeves for around-the-office informality. For women it's a little more difficult. The first rule is to dress your age. The suit, without tie, of course, can be a standard for women, too. But shedding a jacket and rolling up shirt sleeves aren't feasible choices to mark in-office informality for women executives. Shedding the jacket may be the only choice to achieve informal comfort.

## Reevaluate

It's next to impossible to evaluate your career status without reevaluating your career plan. Mike Duncan, although not in the advertising business, offers some "very important principles of career planning" that are applicable to seeking advancement in advertising in his book, *Reach Your Goals in Spite of the Old Boy Network: A Guide for African American Employees.*

- Don't be afraid about making a wrong decision for a career choice. You can always adjust courses. Some people, he says, are afraid to make a firm career choice because "they are afraid it may turn out to be the wrong one. They do not know where they're going so they never get there."
- Decide whether you want to be a manager or a specialist. "Most managers," Duncan says, "are managers because they were good specialists or technicians rather than being good at dealing with people." Also, there are more and better opportunities for good specialists than for managers.
- Learn good project management skills. "Be ready for the day that [you learn] you are needed to work on a special project team. Being a part of a successful project team is one of the quickest ways to make a name for yourself and get you high-level exposure," Duncan says.
- Do not lose sight of your goal, but be ready to change courses temporarily, if necessary. Duncan says that in business there's never a straight line to anything, which is equally true in advertising. The point, of course, is to embrace taking a side road now and then, study the scenery while you're there, but stay aware of other roads that will take you where you want to go.

## Getting Off on the Right Foot Is the First Step up the Mountain

Have you picked out the ladder you want to climb? Creative? Media? Sales? An account position? Traffic? Production? Finance and accounting?

Try this. It's recommended from the early personal experience of advertising veteran Ray Champney. Go around to every department head in the agency. Ask for an overview of how the department operates, what its philosophy is, and how you, in your present capacity, can best help make their jobs easier. You'll learn things you never knew no matter how long you've been in the business.

"The response I'd get across the board was overwhelming. But even more important, the department heads were happy to tell me that I would short circuit a lot of the learning processes I'd have had to go through on my own if I'd skipped this process." Count on it—you'll gather respect, cooperation, and endorsements.

Another way to learn about the business and to be successful in it is to constantly evaluate others' advertising. The pros do it continually. Not only do you keep abreast of what's hot, you can use this strategy to increase the effectiveness of your campaign. When you're home and watching television, or you're out shopping, or when you're just doing weekend activities, you develop an awareness of things that are going on about you that have a relationship to what you're involved in in the work process.

Champney explains,

> That means, for example, if you're involved in media, you will be constantly evaluating when you read the newspaper, look at magazines, watch TV commercials, how these advertisers' messages fit their products or services, according to who their target audience is. Just as the professionals do, you'll absorb and store these evaluations then reapply the knowledge to your own client's needs—whether you're working within the creative area, in the media selection area, or directly with the client.

"It's not fully understood, even within the industry," says Champney, "that to fully participate in this industry there's need for complete understanding and comprehension of all the areas within the business. And it's the individual's responsibility to become involved and learn as much as possible."

Large agencies understand this need, and they previously provided training programs and on-the-job training. It's seldom offered anymore, however, because of the desire and sometimes the need for leaner and meaner agencies. These days, it's each person's individual responsibility to do their own on-the-job training.

## Where You Can Go in an Agency

"You can go crazy!" a lot of people will tell you. But that's only true if you're in the wrong business. Or with the wrong agency. Or in the wrong area within the business.

Consider this fact as you evaluate. Although, to a point, you can move up within an agency, 95 percent of the time to make the quantum leap to the next higher level, you'll have to change agencies.

You may rise within the framework of a very vertical position to the pinnacle of whatever the area is. But if you want to go beyond that point, it's imperative that you make the effort to educate yourself, participate with the others in the agency, and be aware that you are somebody who has a much broader scope than the very vertical line you were hired for. Another bit of counsel from Ray Champney. "If you look on a place in the advertising industry as a job—and that's what you're dedicated to performing—you're not going to go anywhere."

There's an area within an advertising agency that is seldom thought of as a part of the advertising business—finance and accounting. As Ray Champney says, "Advertising is a very creative business. But without the money you can't do anything." It's undoubtedly as important as any area within the field. Just making sure the money comes in on time and is disbursed to the right people in the proper amounts is critical to the very survival of the agency.

Think of all the services required for the simplest print ad—from type and graphics to media placement. A major function of an agency is to place advertising—usually an enormous amount—in the media. Unlike many other businesses, an agency is frequently billed by media before they receive payment from the client. Yet, if payment isn't made to media on time, the agency loses its discount. It's obvious, a slow-paying client can mean disaster.

Beyond these operations, there's the responsibility for the agency's payroll, as well as company benefits programs such as medical insurance, retirement plans, and profit-sharing programs.

So, has the point been made? Finance and accounting is an important, prestigious department that's worthy of consideration by those who have the smarts to learn it and the temperament to love it.

## Job Postings? Not Likely

Many businesses post, in one form or another, announcements of forthcoming and existing unfilled positions within the company. This is not a regular practice among agencies.

There may be certain government rules and regulations about hiring practices that the agency will follow. But advertising is very much an individual business, based on performance that is not as easily measured as it is in other businesses. So, identifying someone who might have the talent to fill a certain slot isn't easily done with a piece of paper.

Agency executives know their people well enough to know whether there's anyone capable of filling a specific slot. And a lot of grooming goes on within the organization. A qualified person is moved into the spot, and a new person is brought in for the lower position.

## THINKING ABOUT MOVING TO A CORPORATE ADVERTISING DEPARTMENT?

In an advertising agency the word *"CLIENT"* is spoken in italic capitals. And when it's the client who speaks, everyone jumps through hoops. Without clients there is no agency, no work, no income.

So what would you think about working for an agency that IS the client? Working for a company that does its own advertising? Before you say yes—or no—consider the differences.

An *agency* has a broad spectrum of businesses for which it performs. Although it may be narrow in category, it's broad in the numbers of businesses it works for. For example, a business-to-business agency may specialize in designing campaigns to sell ball bearings, wrenches, batteries—each for different clients. It's broad in its spectrum but focused in a category—a business-to-business category—which calls for a variety of different types of business advertising.

Other agencies may specialize in a variety of consumer products. Smaller agencies may have specialty mixes, such as medical, travel and leisure, or hospitality.

In all cases within an agency, the operations are broad in types, thinking, and application, which offer its staffers greater opportunities for expanded thinking, creativeness, and stimulation.

An *in-house operation* is very focused and very vertical in relation to its particular product category. It has a single focus with only the company's own product, service, or image on the table. For example, Southland Corporation does nothing but advertise 7-11 stores. Toys R Us handles only retail advertising and promotional programs for the Toys R Us chain. It's an entirely different environment, and its functions are considerably different. Instead of working with and for multiple clients, in-house ad departments perform functions as dictated by management.

There's another big difference. If you are sure you want a career in *advertising*, but you also want to climb the ladder, an in-house department may not be the place for you for the simple reason that the further up the ladder you climb in a corporation, the farther away from advertising you move.

There are incentives to join a corporate ad department. One is the elimination of the fear of losing clients, which heightens job security. The constant struggle to achieve client approval of ideas or projects is also deleted. There often are pay incentives, too. Salaries tend to be higher than in agencies.

On the less attractive side for those who are creative types is the ongoing need for budgets, fiscal reports, and evaluations. A corporate ad department is more heavily administrative and more structured. Let's just say, if you lean more toward the structured ways of business, but you enjoy the challenges of advertising, this may be the way for you to go.

There's another negative to working in some corporate ad departments whose advertising is handled by an agency. The corporate crew are just administrators who merely review an agency's work and pay the bills. Before planning such a change, you should thoroughly check the way the in-house operation you're considering works.

One of the most attractive pluses of this type of work is that those in a corporate advertising department set the advertising goals and policy for the company—with upper management's approval, of course. If an agency is involved, the corporate department is the link between the two, and it's the corporate department's job to update the agency on product or service developments and the thinking and concerns of top management.

Some corporate departments mirror the agency structure. These advertising departments include creatives, media people, and researchers. In this case, if an agency is involved, the work may be divvied up between the agency and the in-house operation.

One thing both operations have in common is that those employed work hard—very hard. However, for agency people the work tends to come like major winter storms—when it arrives everyone's snowed in. But then the storm lets up a bit, as a rule. With corporate advertising, on the other hand, unless an agency is doing a major part of the work, there's no let-up in the storm. It's business every day, 10, 12, or more hours every day.

## Tips for Joining an In-House Operation

Even though the structure is different between agencies and corporate ad departments, the people who work there have many of the same kinds of qualifications and training, except for one thing: an MBA from a top business school is a necessity, unless you have impressive previous experience and credentials *in manage-ment.*

Buttoned-down thinking—and looks—are also important to give assurance you can and will fit in, even with those in other divisions of the corporation. Professionalism is an important image to convey, and clothes help make the person here, as well as add assurance on a personal basis.

## A "Clothes Encounter"

We interrupt these tips to stress the importance of clothes, in the corporate landscape.

In an eight-panel strip, "Stan Mack's True Tales," the importance of dressing the part is stated with humor:

Panel 1. The strip's leading character, a woman, says, "At work, I was usually insecure, self-conscious, and easily intimidated."

Panel 2. "Then my sister, the fast-track corporate executive, gave me one of her Armani suits."

Panel 3. "In my beautiful new suit—soft and drapey, yet polished and professional—I became calm, confident, and armored."

Panel 4. "I was finally prepared to challenge a co-worker who was using me as a doormat."

Panel 5. "My suit and I went eyeball to eyeball with him in front of my boss."

Panel 6. "With another suit on, I might have wilted, but I was no longer a passive petunia. He blinked first!"

Panel 7. "Now, no one pushes me around at work. And the big cheeses smile at me."

Panel 8. "Because my suit has changed me into quality goods."

No need whatsoever for your suit to have such an impressive name brand. Just as long as it's "polished and professional," you'll not only make a professional impression, but you'll also become "calm, confident, and armored."

## Back to Tips

Now back to the subject of "professionalism." Professionalism for the job contender also includes a strong familiarity with the corporation's products or services, its reputation, its background and history, and knowledge of any recent news about the company as well as about a product or service.

Many corporations prefer to promote from within, so you may want to think several times after joining a corporate ad department before making plans to leave. It's not unusual, however, for people to move back and forth between agencies and corporations. Don't count out going for such a move because you're not yet sure it's the place for you. You can always go back to where you're most comfortable.

## JOINING A SUPPORT GROUP

Now this is a whole different world. It's a world of independents and freelancers who may not get out of their nighties or pajamas when they go to work each morning. Media buying, production, research, copywriting, and account planning are examples of core groups/support groups.

Let's say you've worked within the framework of an agency, and you've achieved expertise in the agency of a popular support field— media buying or research, for example. You're comfortable in that area, and you're interested in going beyond it. You also realize you could make a good living if you become really skilled at it.

You've also recognized there are definite limitations for advancement where you are, whether it's in an agency or a corporation. This is when you may decide to go out on your own.

*On your own?*

Yes, initially you're on your own, looking to join a support team that makes itself available to smaller organizations that don't have the wherewithal to carry that kind of overhead. Essentially, that's what it's all about.

The first thing you'd do is to try the obvious resources: AAAA, the *Red Book*, and the Yellow Pages, to see who's in the marketplace. Look for agencies that don't have a full complement of staff, and pay particular attention to agencies that have downsized and now contract out the kind of work you do. And look for smaller agencies with limited budgets. Companies with in-house ad departments also are potential clients. Then you make them aware that you are now available for your specific support service. That's just a starting point.

You really don't want to be totally on your own. You would like to join an established group. Is that possible? Maybe down the road when you've proven your worth. Initially, probably not, because there aren't many such groups, and those that are around are established. When they add someone to their group, it's someone they already know. Unless, of course, the agency or in-house department you've worked for uses resource groups. That's a special opportunity to make contact and build a relationship as you develop their interest in your abilities, your talents, your worth to them.

In the beginning, it usually amounts to establishing your own independent business as a freelancer, with all the responsibilities for getting the word out about your availability and for marketing yourself. Advertising agencies and corporate ad departments then become your clients.

One way is to tie up with an organization specializing in your field. Media people have their own organizations. Production managers also have their special groups.

Every city has an ad club, and within the ad club there are subgroups. There is a possible problem, though. In these groups there are people in the same capacity vying with each other—copywriters vying with other copywriters, and so forth.

## TAKE A HIKE! IN POSITION, IN PAY

This is where politics gets in the act. Although most career advancement tactics are *not* highly political (most depend on basic time-honored strategies), using winning office politics can still build effectiveness.

Your choice about whether to appear indispensable is purely political. Few people are *actually* indispensable, but if you can make the bosses believe you cannot be replaced, your career rating will climb. The secret here is to gather and maintain valuable contacts and to be more knowledgeable than your peers.

Another tactic that works is for top management to believe you are in demand by other agencies or corporate departments. Of course it can work against you, too. You could be perceived as being so indispensable doing what you're doing that you won't be considered for advancement in either position or pay.

If you're building such a wall of wonder about yourself, perhaps you should think about establishing your effectiveness as strongly as possible, while not cultivating the feeling that there's no one else who can do as good a job as you.


## READY TO CALL IT SPLITS?

Failure may be the best thing that ever happens to you! Don't set your mark to fail. But if your first efforts to move up, around, or out of the ad business don't achieve immediate success, it may be a blessing.

Years back, *Fortune* magazine carried an article by Patricia Sellers that told of the great fortune that came to such people as Walt Disney and Henry Ford, who saw their "ventures end up in bankruptcy before they made it big time." She also told how Sergio Zyman was hired by Coca-Cola to reverse its decline. He came in, dreamed up a new product, and labeled it "New Coke," which ultimately became "the most disastrous new product launch since the Edsel." A year later, Zyman was out of Coca-Cola.

End of story? No way. Seven years later he was back at Coke with his job expanded.

The secret of his "success" was that he didn't close any doors. He went on to start a highly successful consulting company and, eventually, even Coca-Cola sought his advice—then invited him back.

In the *Fortune* article, psychologist Robert Staub is quoted as saying he believes the number one cause of failure is a lack of self-awareness. "You must step outside your skin to adopt the viewpoint of others."

Sellers's final advice is, "If you haven't failed yet, for the benefit of your career you probably should." Remember these words each time you want to make a move—up, around, or out—but are afraid you might not quite hit the target. In other words, stop the navel-gazing—and do something!

## PACK YOUR GEAR FOR THE CLIMB TO ELECTRONIC ADVERTISING

News is a primary attraction in bringing consumers to advertising on the Internet, and it also has a major allure for advertisers. The stats are stunning. At the Web sites of MSNBC, USA Today, CNN, and ABC, online readers in early 1998 accessed a total of more than 700 million pages of news and features each month. This is an audience that did not exist in 1996.

These stats, and the fact that the Internet is the fastest-growing major new medium in the history of the news and information industry, were presented at *Editor & Publisher*'s Interactive Newspapers 1998 conference. Beyond this intriguing information, the *Wall Street Journal* has some pretty impressive figures of its own. It boasts more than 175,000 subscribers who pay $7.5 million a year to access instant business news from its Interactive Edition. According to sources at the *Journal*, advertising accounts for about 60 percent of the site's total revenue. "The Internet is changing the news business in fundamental ways," those attending the conference were told. Surely, they and everyone who reads a newspaper can equate that to advertising. The Internet is changing the advertising business in fundamental ways, too.

There should be a motto for *anyone* in—or hoping to break into, move up, or move around in—the advertising or news business today: Know or Go! Before you even begin packing your climbing gear, be sure you're Net savvy.

The channels for advertising are increasing and changing, but the bottom line is, the future of advertising is strong. So, pack your climbing gear and *be ready* for all the changes. Be ready to make your move—into, up, or around!

# index